For more than forty years,
Yearling has been the leading name
in classic and award-winning literature
for young readers.

Yearling books feature children's
favorite authors and characters,
providing dynamic stories of adventure,
humor, history, mystery, and fantasy.

Trust Yearling paperbacks to entertain,
inspire, and promote the love of reading
in all children.

Published by Yearling, an imprint of Random House Children's Books,
a division of Random House, Inc., New York

Visit us on the Web! www.randomhouse.com/kids

Educators and librarians, for a variety of teaching tools, visit us at
www.randomhouse.com/teachers

*Library of Congress Cataloging-in-Publication Data*
Recycle this book : what you can do to save the world! / edited by Dan Gutman.
— 1st yearling ed.
p. cm.
ISBN 978-0-385-73721-0 (pbk.)
[1. Environmental protection—Citizen participation—Juvenile literature.]
I. Gutman, Dan.
TD171.7.R43 2009
640—dc22
2008010800

Printed in the United States of America

March 2009

10 9 8 7 6 5 4 3 2 1

First Edition

# RECYCLE THIS BOOK

## 100 TOP CHILDREN'S BOOK AUTHORS TELL YOU HOW TO GO GREEN

### EDITED BY DAN GUTMAN

WITHDRAWN

A Yearling Book

# CONTENTS

## PART TWO: YOUR SCHOOL

# FOREWORD

I was thinking—what's the biggest problem facing the world?

Terrorism? Poverty? Drugs? Crime?

No. In my opinion, the biggest problem facing the world is the world itself. Because if we mess up this planet, none of those other problems is going to matter.

Well, I hate to tell you this, but we are messing up this planet.

You've heard a lot about global warming, the energy crisis, oil dependency, melting ice caps, stranded polar bears, rain forests being burned, species becoming extinct, droughts, floods, forest fires, and hurricanes. This is scary stuff. We've got to do something.

You've got to do something.

Maybe you're thinking, *I didn't cause these problems. Why do I have to solve them?*

I'll tell you why. In a decade, more or less, you're going to be a young adult. You'll have plenty of responsibilities because it will be your world. The people who brought on all these problems (that would be my generation and my parents' generation) might not be around to fix them.

Have you ever gone camping? If you haven't, you need to know that you're supposed to leave the campsite in better condition than it was when you arrived. Earth is our campsite. Sorry to say, but your grandparents and parents have not taken very good care of Earth. Your generation needs to clean up the mess, because there's no other campsite.

The good news is, there's a solution to our environmental problems. In fact, there are hundreds of solutions—right here in your hand. Lots of grown-ups care deeply about this planet, and many of them just happen to be the authors of books you know and love. I contacted a hundred children's book authors and asked them what they do to save energy, reduce waste, or help the environment. This book features the words of those authors.

Some of the essays are serious. Some are funny. Some are angry. All are interesting and useful. And after you finish reading them, it's time to act. You are going to be part of the group that changes the world.

*Me? What can I do?* is probably what you're thinking. I know. When you're a kid, you sometimes feel powerless in a world run by grown-ups. It's hard to stay up past your bedtime or get your allowance raised.

But kids can change the world.

Years ago, kids organized on college campuses and helped

focus attention on ending the Vietnam War. And college kids were also involved with the invention of the personal computer and started Microsoft and Google. Young people fight our wars. Teenagers create our music. Kids determine what kinds of television shows get popular, and which movies, too. Kids *make* a difference.

Believe it or not, politicians do listen to citizens. Business leaders do listen to customers. Teachers do listen to students. And parents do listen to children.

When you were younger, your parents taught you how to ride a bike, how to tie your shoes, and how to catch a ball. Now it's up to you to educate them. Kids often teach their parents how to use computers, cell phones, DVD players, and other technologies so many adults find baffling. Parents need to be taught about the environment the same way. And kids are the ones who need to teach them.

You need to talk to your parents and discuss how to conserve gas, save energy, and reduce waste. You need to tell your representative in Congress to pass laws that reward cities and companies for switching to renewable sources of energy. You need to punish companies and governments that cut down rain forests, pollute air and water, drive animals and plants to extinction, and threaten the very existence of the human race.

Don't say *It's impossible! The job is just too big!*

Think again. When I was five years old, President John F. Kennedy gave a speech in which he challenged America to send a person to the moon within ten years. It sounded impossible at the time. We hadn't even been into space yet. But Kennedy's words captured the imagination of the country. A massive national effort was undertaken, and eight years later, Neil Armstrong put his foot on the moon and said, "That's one small step for a man, one giant leap for mankind."

Now we need to undertake another massive national effort. America needs to switch from fossil fuels to renewable sources of energy. That would be an even bigger leap for humanity than stepping on the moon was. And it can be done.

*How?*

First by changing attitudes, and then by changing laws.

Attitudes can change. When I was a kid, there were still places in America where black and white people were not allowed to drink from the same water fountain. You can believe that because you've studied our history in school. There were separate hotels, restaurants, and bathrooms for different races.

Our country isn't perfect today, but we've made some progress. Attitudes about prejudice and discrimination have dramatically changed, and laws have changed along with them. Attitudes and laws about the environment can change, too, and kids can lead the way.

*What can I do?*

Educate your parents. Most grown-ups don't realize how serious our environmental problems are. They're busy with their jobs, trying to put food on the table for you every day.

They may be caring for your grandparents, too. It's not as easy as it looks being a parent.

But you know how serious the world's problems are, because you're reading this book. Your parents care deeply about you and your future. If you tell them that something is important to you, they will listen.

Talk to them about the ideas in these pages. Insist that taking action is vital. The next time your mother tells you to clean your room, tell her you will when she helps clean up the atmosphere.

We all need to change our attitude. When we turn on the TV, we're bombarded by commercials that give the impression our lives will be better if we buy new toys, cars, shampoos, DVDs, pimple creams, and all kinds of other stuff.

Wrong.

What will truly make our lives better? Clean air to breathe, clean water to drink, and people around the world who aren't homeless, starving, and dying. In fact, scientists have found that once our basic needs (food, shelter, water, clothing) are met, buying things does not make us much happier.

Change is hard. When the automobile was invented, people who made buggies and horse collars didn't want to change. When the computer was invented, the typewriter companies didn't want to change. But they had to.

Human beings are going to have to change, whether we

want to or not. It's just a question of whether we change now, when we still have time, or later, when it may be too late.

If you saw the movie *Titanic*, you know that the ship slammed into the iceberg because the lookouts didn't see it until they were almost upon it. If they had seen the iceberg in the distance, the captain could have steered the ship around it. We are on a collision course with environmental disaster, and we are running out of time to steer around it. We need to begin a program to switch to alternative sources of energy now. Each day we delay will make the switch more difficult.

*What's it going to take?*

It's going to take you and your generation to change the world.

As you leaf through this book, some of these suggestions might seem like a drop in a bucket. It's true that you're not going to save the world by giving up plastic bags and carpooling to school. But if *350 million* people give up plastic bags and start carpooling to school, it will make a real difference.

How do we get 350 million people to change? Here's what we need to do. After you finish reading this book, don't stick it on a shelf. Tell three of your friends about it. If you tell three friends, and they tell three friends, and they tell three friends, forty kids will get the message. And if they tell three friends and they tell three friends and they tell three friends, 1,093 kids will get the message.

If that happens just six more times, more than three-quarters of a million kids will get the message. And if they tell their friends . . . well, you get the idea. It's crucially important that every kid get the message.

All your life, grown-ups have been saying that you can accomplish anything you put your mind to. Here's your chance to prove it.

—Dan Gutman, 2009

**DAN GUTMAN** is the author of *Honus & Me*, *The Kid Who Ran for President*, *The Homework Machine*, *The Million-Dollar Shot*, the My Weird School series, and many other books. He lives in Haddonfield, New Jersey.

# PART ONE
# YOUR HOME

**DID YOU KNOW?**

• The total yearly waste produced by U.S. households would fill enough garbage trucks to line up and reach halfway to the moon.

• Each time you take a shower, you use about nine gallons of water.

• If each person replaced just one lightbulb in their home with an Energy Star compact fluorescent lightbulb (CFL), the total energy saved could light more than 2.5 million homes for another year.

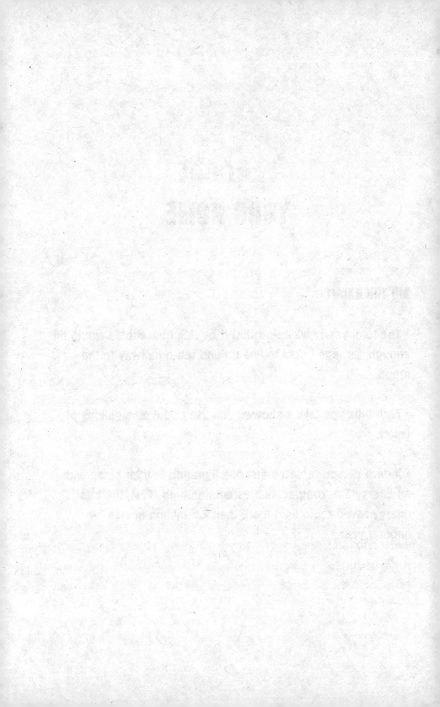

# WHAT DO I DO TO HELP SAVE THE ENVIRONMENT?

## By Seymour Simon

I get my cat, Mittens, to walk on a treadmill to generate electricity. I keep pet alligators to eat the food I waste. I use a magnifying glass to heat my bathwater. I use a stick to write my books on clay tablets. In the summer, I eat only grass. In the winter, I hibernate to save fuel (and eat icicles when I wake up).

Hey, wait! I'm only kidding. Even if I were to get rid of my car, stop using my computers, use sunlight to read instead of electric lighting, stop heating my house in winter and cooling it in summer, nothing I can do alone will save the environment. And nothing you can do alone will save the environment. But maybe, just maybe, things that *we* do, thousands and thousands and millions and millions of us, can help to save our environment.

So here are the little things I do that, if enough of us do them, will help to save our environment. The rule is: The less power we use, the more environmentally friendly we are.

I've changed every lightbulb in my house from an incandescent to a CFL (compact fluorescent lightbulb). I've turned down the thermostat in my house in the winter and in my water heater all year long. I've opened windows in hot weather instead of using an air conditioner. I've switched off lights, turned off my computer, and shut down any other electronic device unless I'm using it. I've cut down on paper bills and paper checks by paying my bills online. I walk instead of using my car whenever I can. Most of all, I think about what I'm doing and try to cut down or eliminate doing anything that's wasteful or harmful to the environment.

All of these things sound like doing nothing much, but if we all do them, maybe, just maybe, we can all help save our environment.

**SEYMOUR SIMON** is the author of more than 250 books for children about science, ecology, nature, and the environment. He is the recipient of many awards, including the first-ever Lifetime Achievement Award from the American Association for the Advancement of Science, Science Books, and

Films; and the Empire State Award for Excellence in Literature for Young People.

## WHAT YOU CAN DO!

Every time you leave the house, turn off the lights, the TV, the computer—anything electronic that doesn't need to be running. Saving a little bit of electricity now will go a long way in your future!

# THE UGLY TRUTH ABOUT SPIT

## By Gennifer Choldenko

Here's the problem with those generic water bottles . . . you buy four of them, you hand them out to the people in the backseat, somebody gets out of the car for a piano lesson, somebody gets in the car from tennis team, somebody switches seats so he can brain his sister because she is just so incredibly annoying—and pretty soon nobody knows whose bottle is whose. And then what happens? C'mon, fess up . . . you've guzzled your sister's spit before, haven't you? Yes. Well, me too. And I want to avoid it. Forever. So here's what I did. I bought sturdy water bottles that I can put in the dishwasher and actually get totally and completely spit free. I wrote each person's name on a bottle and handed it over. It's been days, weeks even, since any spit commingling has happened in our

6

car. Now if I could just think of a good green reason to get my guys to put the toilet seat down.

**GENNIFER CHOLDENKO** is the Newbery Honor–winning author of the *New York Times* bestselling novel *Al Capone Does My Shirts*. She is also the author of *If a Tree Falls at Lunch Period*, *Notes from a Liar and Her Dog*, and *Louder, Lili*.

# A FEW SMALL STEPS

## By Rich Wallace

It's cold outside as I'm writing this, well below freezing in northeastern Pennsylvania. It's cold inside, too, relatively speaking.

I'm wearing a soft, heavy Bucknell University sweatshirt (my son's a student there) with a long-sleeved shirt underneath it. I'm doing that (keeping the heat down and the sweatshirt hood up) because I don't like paying high fuel costs. But I'm also aware that I'm conserving energy, and that's good for the environment.

We do other small things around our house. Instead of filling up the trash can, we keep a separate container for any organic waste like banana peels or onion skins (apple cores go to the dog). You'd be surprised how much that reduces our waste stream. Every other day or so, we dump that stuff in a compost heap in the corner of the yard. It makes great fertilizer for the garden.

For years, we had enormous quantities of plastic supermarket bags filling up cabinet space in our house. A while back, we started bringing our own canvas bags to the store instead. Now we have very few plastic bags.

Maybe all that doesn't sound like much—I certainly wish I was doing more to help the environment—but those are a few of the relatively painless things we do around our house.

**RICH WALLACE** is the author of many novels for teenagers, including *Wrestling Sturbridge* and *Restless: A Ghost's Story*. He also writes the Winning Season series of sports novels for younger kids.

# CONFESSIONS OF A CATALOGAHOLIC

## By Libba Bray

Hi. My name is Libba and I'm a catalogaholic.

Once upon a time, I lived for those pretty, shiny pages full of "stuff." I even got on a mailing list for a doggie outfitter supply company, and I don't have a dog. But I kept getting it on the off chance that I might choose to outfit someone else's dog in a Batman costume. Yeah, any day now.

Not only was I wasting valuable resources with my catalog addiction, I was wasting time, too—time that could have been spent doing something I actually wanted to do, like read, draw, daydream, write, watch a movie, listen to music, learn to juggle, or sing in pig Latin. Well, you get the idea.

One day I stacked the empties—the catalogs I'd finished

off—and, no joke, they took up half of my kitchen floor. I could barely walk to the fridge for a Reese's peanut butter cup, and that is just wrong.

*"Hey!"* I said to myself. "Do you really need all those catalogs? Are you honestly going to order an industrial-sized tin of popcorn or a trout clock whose fins move back and forth in time to 'Burning Love'? And if you are—which I doubt—can't you just order it online?"

So I pulled the plug on my catalog habit. I went to my computer (no paper involved—huzzah!), typed in www.catalogchoice.org, and followed the simple directions. Done. Over. Good-bye! Now my mailbox is lighter. I don't spend hours wrapping those suckers in twine for recycling. And my pig Latin has really improved.

So tell your parents to opt out of the catalog madness. It's a small gesture that makes a huge difference. After all, we need to save that paper for what really matters, like art and secret notes to pass in class, lost-pet flyers, messages in bottles, love letters, and books—things that make life worth living. Things that can't be found in any catalog.

**LIBBA BRAY** is the *New York Times* bestselling author of the books *A Great and Terrible Beauty, Rebel Angels,* and *The Sweet Far Thing.* She lives in Brooklyn, New York, with her husband, their son, their cat, and very few catalogs.

## WHAT YOU CAN DO!

Register yourself and your parents at www.catalog choice.org. And do your shopping online! It's faster and simpler, and there are no rumpled catalogs to dispose of when you're done!

# Hanging out

## By Lois Lowry

Every time guests depart from a visit to my summer home on a Maine hillside and I hang their newly washed sheets out to dry, I find myself thinking: "It's been fun hanging out with you." My stupid private little joke. But the truth is, I love hanging the sheets outside and I love bringing them in, smelling of fresh air and sunshine and breeze. It brings back wonderful memories for me. During my childhood there were no dryers. My mother hung all the laundry outside, and as a toddler I "helped" by handing her the clothespins.

I know that it's ecologically sound to use fresh air instead of electricity. But my reasons for loving the hanging of sheets to dry are much more complex than ecology alone. My reasons have to do with memory, nostalgia, and childhood happiness. If along the way it's good for the environment, too, great. I'm all for it. We should all hang out more often.

**LOIS LOWRY** is a two-time winner of the Newbery Medal, for *Number the Stars* and *The Giver*. She divides her time between Cambridge, Massachusetts, and Bridgton, Maine.

# ONE-YARD PENALTY FOR CLIPPING

## By David Lubar

When I used to mow my lawn (before I found someone who was willing to do this loathsome task for an amazingly reasonable fee), I never bagged the clippings. I would let them lie where they fell so they could decompose and return their nutrients to the soil. (I do the same thing with goldfish, but that's another story.) This actually achieves two good and very green things. First, it doesn't load landfills with bags full of clippings. (While the clippings will decompose, the bags tend to hang around longer than *Law & Order* reruns.) I hate seeing huge stacks of grass-filled bags awaiting the garbage truck. Second, this means I don't need to use fertilizer, which does nasty things to groundwater and puts too much nitrogen in places where it doesn't belong. I have to confess that my reluctance to bag the clippings isn't totally driven by noble reasons. I do tend to be lazy. But it makes me feel good to know that being lazy is sometimes good for the planet.

**DAVID LUBAR** has written all sorts of pollution-free books, including *Hidden Talents* and, appropriately enough, *In the Land of the Lawn Weenies and Other Warped and Creepy Tales*.

# Drinking dog water

## By Peg Kehret

For fourteen years I had a cairn terrier named Daisy. Daisy was a wonderful dog, but her stomach got upset easily. I was vigilant about what she ate and drank.

When my husband and I traveled in an RV to visit schools and libraries, Daisy always came along. We prevented doggy tummy aches by taking water with us, so that the water she drank in campgrounds was the same as what she got at home. We filled gallon jugs with tap water, kept them in the fridge, and used that water for Daisy's bowl whether we were at home or on the road.

One day I asked what everyone at a family gathering wanted to drink with dinner. My son-in-law replied, "I'll have dog water." From then on, any water in my fridge has been known as dog water.

I realized the dog water was as refreshing, tasty, and healthful as a newly opened bottle of water, so I started refilling my small water bottles along with Daisy's jugs.

Eight years ago, when I began doing this, I had a six-pack of bottled water on hand.

I am still drinking from those same six bottles. Once in a while I stick them in the dishwasher, then fill them again from the tap.

I refill my personal bottle about four times a day, which saves the purchase of more than one hundred bottles of water each month. Even if I recycled every bottle, it would take energy to manufacture, fill, and deliver them. 100 bottles a month × 12 months × 8 years = 9,600 bottles! That's 9,600 plastic bottles that I did not buy because I drink dog water, and reuse the bottles, every day.

**PEG KEHRET** is the author of *Earthquake Terror*, *Abduction!*, *Spy Cat*, *Trapped*, and *The Ghost's Grave*, as well as *Small Steps: The Year I Got Polio*.

## WHAT YOU CAN DO!

Buy a reusable water bottle that you can fill up and take wherever you go! Be sure to take this to sports games and other activities where bottled water is being sold—you'll save money and the environment!

# COLD PIZZA FOR BREAKFAST

## By Jane Yolen

You would be amazed at what I eat for breakfast. Cold pizza. Second-day salad. Leftover tuna fish. And when I give a party for friends, I have breakfast stuff for days: deviled eggs, stuffed mushrooms, pâté, carrot sticks, and chopped celery. I also cook something called "compost casserole," which is a silly name for mixing many of my leftovers into a casserole dish, topping it with corn bread batter, and sticking it in the oven till the corn bread has soaked up all the juices and is nicely browned.

When I was little (during World War II), my mother used to make me eat everything on my plate. "Think of the poor, starving Armenians," she would say. And I would grumble to my plate, "Then let's package this up and send it to Armenia, wherever that is."

But to this day, I don't throw food out. Do you know that in America we throw out enough still-eatable stuff to feed many starving populations around the world?

**JANE YOLEN** has written or edited almost three hundred books, including *Owl Moon*, *The Emperor and the Kite*, the Commander Toad series, *Sleeping Ugly*, *The Devil's Arithmetic*, *Dragon's Blood*, and *How Do Dinosaurs Say Goodnight?*

# BE A SUPERHERO

## By Eoin Colfer

What can one person do to save the environment?

In my mind I am that one person and it is up to me, and me alone, to save the planet. Of course this is not true, but I have always had a superhero complex. The greater the challenge, the more I like it.

So what can I do, or more importantly, what am I doing?

Nothing spectacular, actually. Nothing uncomfortable or awkward. To be honest, you can do all you need to do and still live a life of leisure and comfort. How much effort does it take to switch off your TV at night? Or to pop a bottle in a separate bin? Not a whole lot. Buying energy-efficient lightbulbs is hardly slave labor. Crumpling cardboard for the recycler is actually fun, especially if you pretend those kitchen roll tubes are steel bars. I know. I am a sad person. What makes it even sadder is that I do a maniacal laugh as I am crushing the tubes.

Anyway, my point is that saving the environment does not have to be difficult. Just adjust your brain a little and live your life a little better. No sweat required. Switch off, unplug, recycle, and laugh maniacally all the while.

**EOIN COLFER** lives in Ireland and is the author of the Artemis Fowl series. His newest book is *Airman*.

## WHAT YOU CAN DO!

Make a list with your parents of all the things you do in your home that harm the environment. Then discuss how many of them you can reasonably change, making an effort to use less energy.

# PAPERBACK WRITER

## By Joseph Bruchac

I've been recycling mailing envelopes for thirty years now—big manila envelopes and padded envelopes that are used by my various publishers to send me their latest catalogs.

I never cut envelopes open but always open them carefully at the flap—sometimes the small flap at one end of the envelope has been taped. I keep my mailing envelopes in stacks organized by size till I need one. Then I peel off or black out the old mailing labels and put on a new one. Sometimes I use a stick-on label, sometimes just a white piece of paper that I cut from scrap paper, write the address on, and then tape onto the envelope. Then I put one of the many stickers with my name and address on it in the upper left-hand corner. I get sent labels all the time from the Cousteau Society, the

Wilderness Society, Greenpeace, National Wildlife Federation, etc. We give to lots of environmental groups.

I also keep my waste stream low by reusing paper—making notepads out of paper with print on only one side, such as early drafts of my work that I've printed out. Then, after using both sides, I run the paper through a shredder and compost it. I also shred the junk mail that still comes in.

I compost all our household organic garbage in several forms of composters, from a tumbler to four three-foot-by-three-foot square bins made of concrete blocks. I layer the shredded paper with food waste, grass clippings, shredded leaves (in the autumn), and soil. We have several large organic vegetable gardens and also a lot of fruit trees and berry bushes that benefit from the compost and mulch. We also use our newspapers as the first layer on the earth when we are mulching our gardens, followed by grass clippings or shredded leaves. This past year we covered a few thousand square feet with old issues of *News from Indian Country* and the *Bloomsbury Review*. So we have highly literate fruits and vegetables.

*Olakamigenoka*—Make Peace.

**JOSEPH BRUCHAC**, coauthor of the Keepers of the Earth series, is a writer and storyteller whose work often reflects his Abenaki Indian ancestry and his concerns about the environment.

# TURN IT OFF!

## By Eric A. Kimmel

Want to do something to help our planet and conserve energy? It's easier than you think and doesn't involve any significant change to your lifestyle. Just remember these three words: Turn it off!

Enormous amounts of energy are wasted every day on nothing. I first realized this one morning when I set up our coffee grinder. The plastic cover above the motor was warm. Why should it be warm? I hadn't ground any coffee in twenty-four hours. Then the realization struck me. The motor is on all the time, as long as the grinder is plugged in. Pressing the On button engages the gears and starts the grinder working. In other words, this appliance has been on for hours even though I only use it for less than a minute. Granted, it uses up

25

a tiny amount of energy. But think of this: How many coffee grinders are there like mine? How many are left plugged in all day and all night? Multiply a tiny amount of energy millions of times and you end up with a significant amount of energy being consumed for no purpose at all. From now on, I plug in the coffee grinder only when I'm actually using it. The plug comes out of the socket when I'm done.

The experience with the coffee grinder started me thinking. How else am I wasting energy without even realizing it? Lights, for one. Why should the light be on when no one's in the room? Turn it off! Why should the TV, radio, iPod docking station be on when nobody's listening? Turn it off! What about your computer and its peripherals: printer, hard drives, modem? Granted, there's no point in turning off your system when you're walking away for only a few minutes. But what if it's more than a few minutes? Does the whole system need to be on all night? When you're in school? On vacation? If you don't need to have it on and you're not going to be using it for a while, turn it off!

Here's another secret. I did a little research on the subject and discovered that all the convenient rechargers we have to recharge our laptops, cell phones, wireless phones, iPods, etc., consume electricity even though they're not recharging anything. In other words, if your cell phone is in your pocket, the charger doesn't have to be in the wall. Pull it out! Turn it off! Use it when you need it.

During World War II there was a popular poster that said,

*Is this trip necessary?* Gasoline was rationed and in short supply. So were tires and diesel fuel. Each trip in the car, on the bus, or on the train consumed materials and fuel supplies that were needed for the war effort. If you didn't need to travel, you were supposed to stay home. We ought to remember that poster and ask ourselves, "Does this need to be plugged in? Does this need to be on?"

If the answer is no, turn it off!

**ERIC A. KIMMEL** is the author of more than sixty books for children, including *Anansi and the Moss-Covered Rock* and the 1990 Caldecott Honor Book *Hershel and the Hanukkah Goblins*.

## WHAT YOU CAN DO!

Check your appliances each morning with your parents before you leave for school. Unplug anything that doesn't need to be running all day. Be sure to do this when you leave for a vacation, too!

# Since We Can't Stop Moose From Belching

## By Todd Strasser

First, I think it's important to put things in perspective. We're not the only animals who are messing up the earth's atmosphere. Methane is a major greenhouse gas that contributes to global warming. Here are the top three animal producers of that stuff:

1. Wood-munching termites.
2. Belching moose.
3. Cattle that, er, well, emit a lot of methane gas from you-know-where.

The problem is, we can't do very much about them. You can try, but termites won't listen, you don't really want to get within talking distance of a moose, and cows are too busy chewing their cud.

On the other hand, we *can* do something about the greenhouse gases we help create by using more energy than we need to. Here are three really simple things I do:

1. Open windows. Weird, huh? But I'm amazed at how many people run air conditioners at night when the outside temperature has dipped into the lower seventies or upper sixties. I usually open two windows in two different rooms. In one room I have a fan facing outside so that it blows out hot air and pulls in cool night air through the other window.

2. Wear a sweater indoors in the winter, and a T-shirt in the summer. I know a lot of people who cool their houses to sixty-eight degrees in the summer and warm the same houses to seventy-two in the winter. Imagine how much energy we'd save if we did the opposite and kept our houses at seventy-two in the summer and sixty-eight in the winter. I keep my house around sixty-seven degrees in the winter, which is fine as long as I wear a sweater. In the summer it's reasonably comfortable up to around seventy-five degrees.

3. Ride a bike. Yeah, yeah, I know, it's another no-brainer. But so simple. Whenever possible, I run local errands on my bike. Not when it's raining, and not when the temperature

gets much below sixty degrees. But that's still a lot of days to save energy.

That's it. Just three simple suggestions. And they're all easier than talking to a moose.

When he's not writing, **TODD STRASSER** conserves energy by doing as little as possible.

# CELEBRATE ARBOR DAY!

## By Katy Kelly

I am wild for Arbor Day. You don't have to wrap anything. You can celebrate it early or late if you are too busy on the last Friday of April, which is when it is usually held. And since no one is paying attention to who is naughty and who is nice, you don't even have to be especially well behaved in the days leading up to the holiday. Also, there is only one thing you must do: Plant a tree. Everything else is up to you. I eat chocolate and dance with my dog, Elly. You may decide to stand on your head. Or juggle turnips. Or cook a shoofly pie. Or do nothing at all except plant a tree. Luckily, that one thing is fun and important and can last for the rest of your life.

When I was eight years old, my family planted a damson plum tree in our front yard. When I was grown up and getting married, we planted a fig tree in my parents' backyard. And when my husband and I had a baby, my mom and dad planted a tree. They figured Emily and the tree would get tall and strong together and that one day Emily would be able to climb to the top. They call it a grandchildren tree. Emily and the rest of the grandchildren call it an apple tree.

Those three trees are all still growing, producing fruit and making shade. They are also helping to reduce global warming by taking carbon dioxide out of the atmosphere and putting oxygen into the air. That is such a big deal that now we celebrate Arbor Day whenever we celebrate anything. Christmas trees are bought live and replanted. Friends with new houses get willow trees. New babies get dogwoods. Birthdays are commemorated by hazelnut bushes, and the first day of first grade is remembered with a red oak sapling.

**KATY KELLY** is the author of the Lucy Rose series, as well as *Melonhead*. She is a senior editor at *U.S. News & World Report* and lives in Washington, D.C., with her husband and children.

## WHAT YOU CAN DO!

To learn more or to buy or give a tree, go to www .arborday.org.

# The hoax

## By Gary Schmidt

Gardens, you know, are a hoax.

You go to the hardware store in the spring, and lined up on a neat set of shelves are the Seed Packages. The pictures of fruits and vegetables are so beautiful, you want to cry.

So you buy the seeds. And you plant. And you water. And you nurture. You sing to the doggone things. And a few weeks later, something pops out of the ground that looks nothing like those beautiful pictures on the seed packages.

Half of them immediately are eaten by something with many legs. A few days later, most of the other half will go, too. You'll fight with weeds through a hot August for everything that remains. Some of it will survive.

A garden will break your heart every time.

So maybe the pictures on the seed packages are a hoax. But isn't it more of a hoax to have vast planting operations— I will not say farms—spray our vegetables with pesticides, and to pretend that those chemicals will never enter our bodies?

Isn't it more of a hoax to pretend that the energy put into boating, flying, and trucking fruit from Guatemala to super-markets in Boise, Idaho, is equivalent to the energy we get out of the food?

Isn't it more of a hoax to inject a cow with steroids until it produces gargantuan amounts of milk—slaughtering it a year later when it cannot sustain this unnatural rate—and not to know that those steroids will find their way into us?

A garden is really all we have. It is all we ever have had. The rest is the hoax.

So this fall, I will turn the garden over again by hand, with a spade. And in the spring, I will plant again. I know that what comes up will not look anything like the beautiful pic-tures on the packages. I know I will have to share it with the animals that come by night—and that, by the way, haven't shown any kind of gratitude.

But what I gather, my family will eat. We will take it from the garden just before dinner. The tomatoes will taste like none that have ever been sprayed and trucked and misted and plasticked. The jade beans will snap loudly. The emerald peas will fall from their pods into our open mouths and probably not make it to the table. The potatoes will be soft and white. And the raspberries, plucked from between their thorns, will fall into open palms, as softly as dreams of what may be in a perfect garden.

**GARY SCHMIDT** lives on an old farm in Alto, Michigan, where each spring he plants and struggles with a large fruit and vegetable garden. He is the author of *Lizzie Bright and the Buckminster Boy*, *First Boy*, and *The Wednesday Wars*.

## WHAT YOU CAN DO!

Gather your parents, siblings, grandparents, or friends, and plant a garden in your backyard. You'll have delicious fruits and vegetables just steps from your back door, and you'll have a project to do with the people you care about!

# THERE IS NO MEAT IN CHOCOLATE CAKE

## By Maryrose Wood

I am every grandmother's worst nightmare—the Thanksgiving dinner guest who does not eat turkey.

"But it's Thanksgiving!" I used to hear, before my family finally got used to my eating habits. "You have to eat some turkey!"

No, I did not. And I do not. I've been a vegetarian for nearly twenty-five years now, and during that entire time I've subsisted happily on good healthy vegetarian foods. Like chocolate cake and pizza.

Now, I don't think that everyone should be a vegetarian.

But eating less meat is not only good for your health, it's good for the environment, too.

Why? Think about the cow that turned into the hamburger you ate yesterday. That cow had been eating like—well, like a cow, since the day it was born. Chances are it weighed more than a thousand pounds by the time it was prematurely sent to cow heaven, so you can imagine how many calories it had consumed in its life. Gazillions, I think is the precise answer.

Those calories probably came from commercially grown feed made of corn and soy and lots of additives. The corn and soybeans were most likely grown with the use of tons of chemical fertilizers, much of which ran off into nearby lakes and rivers. Yuck!

The additives might include things like hormones to make the cows fatten up faster and antibiotics to prevent the cows from getting sick from eating the feed. Why does the feed make them sick? you ask. Because cows are designed to graze on grass, not eat weird chemical-laced feed. If you think about that for a while your head will hurt, I promise.

Feeding a cow gazillions of calories just so a roomful of humans can enjoy a steak dinner is an incredibly wasteful way to make food. Someone once figured that twenty vegetarians could live off the land required to feed one meat eater. Reducing our meat consumption even a small amount would free up millions of tons of grain, enough to feed whole nations full of hungry people.

And OMG! Don't forget the trees! Millions of acres of forests have been cut down to make room for cattle grazing. Those forests make oxygen, which is kind of important. The cows make methane-filled burps and farts, which contribute to global warming. It's a no-brainer, people!

I'm picking on cows here, but the same is true for all kinds of animals that are commercially raised for human consumption. And guess what? Everything the cow (or pig, or chicken) ate ends up in that nice hormone-and-antibiotic-flavored meat meal on your plate, and soon in you. Pizza, anyone?

Eating less meat is easy to do, and veggies and grains and legumes are delicious! When you or your parents do shop for meat (or eggs, or even milk), buy products that are not from the big corporate meat-factory world that stuffs animals with feed full of toxic chemicals. Look for labels like "organic," "free-range," "grass-fed," and "no hormones or antibiotics used." It will likely cost a bit more, but you're going to eat less of it, so it will all balance out.

And try to be a vegetarian for a couple of meals (or maybe even a couple of days) a week. The chocolate cake is waiting. . . .

**MARYROSE WOOD** has acted on Broadway, ridden camels in India, and performed improv comedy in New York City nightclubs. She's also the author of the young adult novels *Sex Kittens and Horn Dawgs Fall in Love*, *Why I Let My Hair Grow Out*, and *My Life: The Musical*.

# GREEN AND GRACIOUS

## By Kirby Larson

When our kids were little, my husband and I used a lot of paper napkins and paper towels. Then, when she was in fourth grade, our daughter did a report on the environmental impact of all the paper products we used. It was not pretty! So I went right out and bought cloth napkins, which our family has used ever since (well, I've had to buy new ones now and again, but you get the idea). If you're handy with a needle, you can personalize the napkins with embroidered initials; fabric paint works, too. Every couple of days, I throw the napkins in the laundry. It's an easy and classy way to go green.

True confession: While I haven't completely weaned myself from paper towels, I only use the plain ones because the patterned ones have all those bad inks and dyes. Using cloth napkins and cloth rags is a doubly green habit—it helps reduce waste and it's easier on my budget, leaving me more money to spend on books.

**KIRBY LARSON** is the author of the Newbery Honor–winning book *Hattie Big Sky*.

# THE JOY OF WORM COMPOSTING

## By Ralph Fletcher

I have always been interested in processes of transformation—
how one thing can morph into something else. Once upon a
time there were people known as alchemists who believed you
could turn lead into gold. (Not true, but intriguing.) I had a
rock tumbler that could turn common stones into polished
gems. So when I heard about worm composting, I loved the
idea that common food scraps could be magically turned into
something marvelous and useful.

Here's the basic idea: Instead of throwing away your leftover food, you feed it to a colony of red worms. The worms eat
that stuff and turn it into rich soil you can use for plants or in
your garden.

I purchased some red worms (they look like common

earthworms) from a company in California. The composter I purchased consists of four stacking trays. There are holes in the bottom of each tray so the worms can migrate up or down depending on where the food is. Mine is called an Upwardly Mobile Composter, which I think is funny. (I mean, do these worms hope to move into a richer neighborhood or something?) I started the composter by mixing a "coir" (fibers from the husk of a coconut) with some dirt and shredded cardboard. Then I added the worms and gave them a moderate amount of food.

It worked! The worms eat almost anything, but they especially love coffee grinds, cereal, French fries, greasy pizza cardboard, moldy bread, and spoiled vegetables. You know the glossy flyers you find in Sunday newspapers? That paper is covered with clay, and the worms go wild for it. I shred it and give it to them as a treat. My son once complained: "You treat those worms better than your kids!" That is entirely untrue, though I do bring the composter into the garage during the winter so they don't freeze in the icy New Hampshire air.

The worms eat the food and pass it out the other end of their bodies. This probably sounds pretty gross, but the resulting "soil" is fresh and rich. Try it! Trust me: There's no unpleasant smell at all. You end up with grade-A loam for all your plants and shrubs. Plus you get the satisfaction of reducing the amount of stuff you throw away and, in a small but tangible way, making this Earth a better place.

**RALPH FLETCHER** has written numerous books for young readers, including the memoir *Marshfield Dreams: When I Was a Kid*, *Fig Pudding*, *Flying Solo*, and *The One O'Clock Chop*, a young adult novel. His picture books include *Twilight Comes Twice* and *The Sandman*.

## WHAT YOU CAN DO!

Start composting in your backyard! Block off an area where you can throw away your food scraps, and then use the soil to plant a garden!

# I'M GREEN

## by David A. Adler

I'm green! Lights in my home and office are on only if they're needed, and most lights, including all in my office, which often stay on long into the evening, are fluorescent. The energy used to keep them burning is just a fraction of what incandescent old-fashioned lights use. I use much less paper now than I did thirty years ago when I wrote my first Cam Jansen mystery. Now I type directly onto my computer, rewrite again and again, and sometimes send the manuscript to my editor via the Internet so I don't use paper at all! That saves trees. Oh, and I work where I live. My office is in my home, so I don't drive to work. I walk there, just down some steps and across the hall, and that saves gasoline, which helps our environment. But I don't save calories. My office is just a few steps from the kitchen, so while I'm saving my environment, I take too many snack breaks.

**DAVID A. ADLER** is the author of more than two hundred books for young readers, including the Cam Jansen and Young Cam Jansen Mysteries and the Picture Book Biography series.

# PLUNGER-MAN

## By Gordon Korman

In my house, I'm known as Plunger-Man. I may not be able to leap tall buildings in a single bound, or even figure out how to set the timer on the oven. But when a toilet clogs, I'm your guy.

Here's the thing: When we bought our house, our downstairs bathroom came with the Rolls-Royce of toilets—a real designer job. When the seat cracked, the replacement part alone cost three hundred bucks. I'll never forget what the salesman told me when I expressed my dismay at the price tag: "Sure, it's expensive—but that's a beautiful toilet!" I almost said, "Dude, I'm not planning to display it in my picture window!"

Another problem with my Rolls-Royce—it was just about

the most environmentally unfriendly plumbing fixture on our endangered planet. Seriously, you could irrigate a kibbutz with every flush. Uncounted gallons of wasted water. So we came to a momentous decision—the monster had to go. And we made sure to replace it with a very green model. Not the color—I mean one of those newfangled commodes with turbo-flush technology that uses a thimbleful of water.

And everything was wonderful—until our first clog. That was when Plunger-Man made a stunning discovery. When you're dealing with a bowl the size of Loch Ness, it's a no-brainer to plunge that obstruction halfway to the Arctic Circle. But when a thimbleful of water is all you have to work with, you're moving the clog a thimbleful at a time. Suddenly the sewer line seemed very far away.

Oh, I managed it eventually—after much time and repetitive strain injury. Plunger-Man always gets his clog. I just didn't feel like a superhero anymore. I'll still wield the plunger in the future, but I'm turning in my title and my cape.

Then again, for the environment, it's definitely a small price to pay.

**GORDON KORMAN** is the author of more than sixty books, including *Schooled, Swindle, Gecko,* and *Unleashed.* His long-range plan to help the environment is to get rich, retire, and save the world a whole lot of paper.

# ▌ZAPPED MY TV SET!

## By Bruce Coville

Okay, I didn't actually kill the darn thing. I just use the remote a lot, because I think one of the best things a person can do for the environment is turn off the TV. But not for the reasons you might think. I'm not talking about conserving electricity or anything like that.

Heck, you don't even have to turn the thing off completely.

Just mute it during the commercials.

What good does that do? Well, this one takes a few steps to explain, so stick with me a minute here.

The first thing you have to understand is what television is all about. How do the networks make money? What are they selling?

Off the top of your head you might say, "Well, they're selling their shows. Duh!"

Um, not quite.

If you understand a little more about how the system works, you might say, "Ah, I know! They're selling advertising!"

Close, but no cigar.

Let's look at it the other way around. The people who pay for the shows you see on network TV are indeed the advertisers. And what are those advertisers buying when they pay for a show?

Space in your brain!

When a sponsor pays to have his commercial shown, he gets a promise that in return, that message will go into millions of brains. So what the networks are really selling is an entryway to your head.

Setting aside the fact that I don't like other people making money off my brain, what does this have to do with the environment?

That part is simple. The whole point of advertisements is to get us to buy stuff—most of which we don't need. And if you're a kid, almost all that stuff is made of plastic, which, of course, is a petroleum product. (More money for the oil companies!) The cool thing I discovered when I stopped watching advertisements was that I also stopped wanting so much stuff.

This not only made me happier, it meant I had a smaller environmental footprint.

- It's a twofer!

So zap your TV set, if only with that Mute button. You'll save money and help save the environment at the same time.

**BRUCE COVILLE** has written more than ninety books for young readers, many of them about aliens who look at Earth and wonder how humans ever managed to make such a mess out of such a beautiful planet and whether we're ever going to clean it up.

## WHAT YOU CAN DO!

Spend one less hour watching TV (or playing computer or video games, or surfing the Internet) a day. Spend that time being creative, getting outside, or being with friends and family. You'll save electricity and maybe discover some hidden talents!

# Living in the City

## By Elizabeth Levy

Sometimes when I speak at a school, one of the kids will ask, "What kind of car do you drive?" When I say, "I don't own a car," some kids say, "How can you live!"

I live in a city. I love the city. Living in a city is actually good for the environment. When some people think of cities, they think of a lot of garbage and pollution. But a lot of us city dwellers don't have cars and don't use gas. For example, I ride my bike or take the subway. Nobody has to heat my house. I live in an apartment building with a few hundred people, so we all share one boiler. I pick up after my dog . . . and now I even put the waste in biodegradable bags.

But I have a guilty secret: I like to use paper plates. I love to have my godchildren, nieces and nephews, and now great-nieces and great-nephews all stay with me, but I don't love cleaning up. I have never loved cleaning up. My nieces and nephews *hate* when I use paper plates. "It's hurting the environment!" they shout at me. Well, they don't shout, but they do tease me about it.

So we compromise. They clean up. And my niece gave me a set of bowls with a built-in straw. I (or my great-nephews and great-nieces) can now eat cereal and drink milk out of the same bowl. It's only one thing to clean! It's great for the environment, and fun. And so are cities!

**ELIZABETH LEVY** has written more than eighty books, including *Big Trouble in Little Twinsville*, *The Principal's on the Roof*, *Tackling Dad*, *Seventh Grade Tango*, and *Night of the Living Gerbils*.

# Be Passive!

## By Gail Gibbons

Everybody knows you can put solar panels up on your roof to capture the energy of the sun. But up here in Vermont, our family uses the power of the sun in another way: We use passive solar energy.

Passive solar energy is sunlight converted to heat without mechanical equipment. My husband, Kent, built our home in 1978. The house faces south, with nothing blocking the sun. There are hills on the north, east, and west to protect our house from cold winds. We have 240 square feet of thermal-pane windows, and almost all of them face south. During the winter months, the sun shines low in the horizon, so it comes through the windows at a very sharp angle. When it is sunny and eight degrees outside, it feels perfectly comfortable in here. The best part is that on sunny days we don't burn any fuel to heat the house at all. When we do have to turn on the heat, our chimney is in the center of the house, so the heat radiates in all directions.

Nobody expects you to go out and build a new house. But you can use passive solar energy, too. On sunny days in the winter, open the curtains and shades in the rooms of your house when the sun shines through those windows. On sunny days in the summer, close the curtains and shades according to where the sun is in the sky. You'll use less heat in the winter and less air-conditioning in the summer.

**GAIL GIBBONS** is the author/illustrator of *Recycle!: A Handbook for Kids* and more than a hundred other nonfiction books.

# WRONG CENTURY

## By Debbie Dadey

Sometimes I feel like was born in the wrong century. Maybe that's why I love writing about past times in *Cherokee Sister*, *Whistler's Hollow*, and the Ghostville Elementary series (the ghosts were from a hundred years ago). Sometimes I use candles just for the fun of it. After all, candles save energy, give off light and heat, and look so pretty. It's neat to see what it would have been like in the old days, living just by candlelight. I know candles can be dangerous (there's that pesky risk of burning something down!), so make sure you use them wisely with your parents' permission. Another way to try living in the past is to turn off electricity more often. Do we really need to turn on lights in the daytime? Probably not.

Let's turn off the lights, save energy, and live like people did a hundred years ago!

**DEBBIE DADEY** is the author of *The Worst Name in Third Grade* and the Swamp Monster Series and coauthor of the Bailey School Kids series.

# My House Has Vampires!

## By Megan McDonald

Hey, kids! Judy Moody is not the only one who can save the world. Saving the earth starts one person at a time.

I usually begin a book by scribbling ideas on a napkin. So next time you go to throw something away, stop and think: Maybe it has another use. My husband has the world's largest collection of twist ties. I'm sure we'll find a use for them someday!

Stuff I've rescued from the curbside trash: Coffeepot. Desk lamp. Pencil sharpener. Hangers. Books. Chair. Flowerpots. I even found a trash can in a trash can!

Last year, my husband and I bought a new old house. Yep. You heard right. Our whole house is recycled! The cherrywood for the floors came from another house that was torn own. The wood trim around the doors and windows came from old redwood barrels. Even the light fixtures are from old houses. Our house doesn't have a dishwasher (except me!), which saves a lot of water and energy. It doesn't have a fireplace that pollutes the air. But it does use solar energy to help heat the house, and we wear comfy sweaters a lot in the winter.

We have five gardens where we grow organic vegetables. Call me Human Sluggo, because I spend a lot of time pulling up those gross, disgusting, slimy slugs by hand. This way, we don't have to spray our veggies with toxic chemicals that will go into the water supply, then the river, then the ocean.

Speaking of water, where I live in California it rains *a ton* in the winter and *not a drop* in the summer. So guess what? If you put out ginormous rain barrels, you can catch rainwater and save it to water the garden in the summer. Pretty cool, huh?

Recently I learned that my house has vampires! Not the blood-sucking kind that you chase away with garlic. The kind that use up energy from all the stuff we plug in (computers, cordless phones, cell phone chargers) even when we're not using it. This uses the same amount of energy that it would take *five* nuclear power plants to produce. What a waste! Plug everything into a power strip, and turn that off when you're not using it.

My new kick is to download music instead of buying CDs. Discarded CDs are piling up in our landfills. I read that one million of those things would equal three Empire State Buildings!

**MEGAN MCDONALD** is the author of the *New York Times* bestselling Judy Moody series, which includes *Judy Moody Saves the World*. She also wrote *Stink: The Incredible Shrinking Kid* and other books about Judy Moody's pesky little brother.

## WHAT YOU CAN DO!

Talk to your parents about making your home environmentally friendly. Do you have energy-saving appliances? Do you recycle? Do you use natural cleaning products? Have a family meeting about all the small changes you can implement in your own home that will make big changes in the world.

# GREEN . . . AND GREENER

## By Cynthia DeFelice

Hey, kids? Want to be green? Drive a hybrid vehicle like mine! They use less gas, and that is a good thing for the planet.

Oh . . . you say you can't drive? Good point.

Okay, then. Here's my tip: Stay a kid! That way you'll never drive at all, let alone drive a big gas guzzler of a car.

Oh . . . you say you don't want to remain a child? You want to grow up? Okay. I admit it; that's a pretty good point.

Okay, then. Here's my tip: Harass your parents into driving a hybrid car! They will use less gas, and that will be a good thing for the planet.

Oh, you already did that? Good for you. Congratulations. What did you say? You say I could start riding a bicycle like yours? It won't use any gas at all, and that's an even better thing for the planet?

You know . . . you've got a point there. Thanks for the tip!

**CYNTHIA DEFELICE** writes novels for middle-grade readers, including spooky mysteries like *The Ghost of Fossil Glen* and *The Missing Manatee* and dramatic historical fiction like *Weasel* and *The Apprenticeship of Lucas Whitaker*. She also writes picture books, among them *One Potato, Two Potato* and *Old Granny and the Bean Thief*.

# Your Pick

## By Gail Carson Levine

When it is time for you to own your first car, I suggest you get a hybrid or whatever technology is around then that uses the least gas—but only if you are emotionally strong.

I drive a hybrid, and I love it. The mileage is incredible. I rarely have to tank up. I'm richer, which makes me and my husband happy. And of course our Airedale, Baxter, who could power a generator all by himself, is proud of us.

Alas, I pay a sad price. Whenever our car is turned off, it rates the driver's performance in terms of fuel efficiency. If the driver has done well, "Excellent!" appears on the dashboard's little screen. If the driver has done spectacularly well, the readout is "Excellent! Excellent! Excellent!" However, if the driver has not impressed the car, silence reigns.

Whenever my husband drives, even if he only backs the car out of our driveway, he gets at least an "Excellent!" Theoretically, the electric energy kicks in when the driver brakes, so braking is good. And going easy on the gas pedal is good. Now, I believe I brake as much as anybody, and my foot on the gas pedal is not made of lead, but when I drive, I get no *Excellent!*'s. I get zip from my beloved car. Still, I am tough. My broken heart mends itself over and over. Instead, I take my kudos from the dollars I save and from the thought that I am doing this eensy-teensy thing for the environment.

If your feelings are easily hurt, if you can't take a little snubbing from an inanimate object, I think you should buy a gas guzzler. It will never turn its nose up at you. Your wallet will be lighter, too—less drag in your purse, less bulge in your hip pocket. So, when the time comes, you decide.

**GAIL CARSON LEVINE** is the author of *Ella Enchanted,* which won a Newbery Honor. She lives and drives in New York's Hudson Valley.

# THE GARBOLOGIST

## By Matt Tavares

My father-in-law, Woody Freeman, is a garbologist. Technically, he's the transfer station supervisor in Wiscasset, Maine. But he prefers the title *garbologist*, probably because it's more fun to say.

Really, the term *garbologist* is pretty accurate. A garbologist studies a society by analyzing its garbage. As transfer station supervisor, Woody gets to see firsthand exactly how much stuff people are throwing away. And one thing he's learned in his daily role: People throw away too much stuff.

As you might imagine, Woody is very careful about what he throws away. He has mastered the art of reducing, reusing, and recycling. My favorite example of this happened a couple of years ago when my in-laws needed a new dining room floor. Around the same time, my wife and I were thinking about getting a fence for our yard.

The garbologist had an idea.

When Woody pulled up the old floorboards, he was careful not to break them. He brought them out to his workshop and cut them into thirty-inch sections. Then he rounded off one end of each section. And just like that, an old dining room floor was ready to become a brand-new picket fence. Woody loaded all the pickets into his truck and brought them to our house. We all helped build the fence; then my wife and I painted it white. Looking at the fence today, you'd never guess that it used to be a dining room floor.

Before you throw something away, whether it's a piece of scrap paper or an entire dining room floor, ask yourself: Does this need to be thrown away? Would the garbologist throw this away? Could I recycle it? Could someone use it for something?

Be your own garbologist!

**MATT TAVARES** has written and illustrated several picture books, including *Lady Liberty: A Biography* (written by Doreen Rappaport), *Mudball*, and *'Twas the Night Before Christmas*.

*In memory of Woody Freeman*

## WHAT YOU CAN DO!

Can your family reduce the amount of trash they produce in a week? Give it a try! If you create two bags of trash per week normally, see if you can reduce that to one.

# ZEUS SAYS: ZAP THIS!

## By Rick Riordan

Saving the environment would be so much easier if I were a Greek mythological character. If I were a satyr like Grover (in my Percy Jackson and the Olympians novels), I wouldn't have to worry about recycling cans and bottles. I'd just eat them. If I were Dionysus, I could grow all the new plants I wanted just by waving my hand. Of course, they'd all be grapevines, but nobody's perfect. If I were Poseidon, I could take care of all these rising ocean levels caused by global warming. And if I were Zeus, I'd threaten with my lightning bolts until world leaders got serious about changing our laws to protect the earth!

Alas, I'm just one mortal. What can one regular human do to make a difference?

Actually, a lot. My sons are big video gamers, and here's one idea they came up with to help the environment: Use rechargeable batteries.

For years in our house, we were always scrounging around for double-A or triple-A batteries. We never seemed to have enough. The Wii remotes needed them. The wireless mouse and keyboard needed them. The flashlights we use for trick-or-treating, the electronic Halloween and Christmas decorations that light up and make noise, even the cat toys needed batteries! The thing is, those batteries are full of horrible acid, heavy metals, and other stuff that would make even a satyr sick to his stomach. When they get thrown away and go into a landfill, it's bad news for the environment. Replacing them all the time also gets really expensive.

Then Zeus, the god of lightning, zapped us with this new idea for making electricity. We bought a battery charger and rechargeable batteries instead of the throwaway kind. You can find them at most grocery stores. It cost us a few extra dollars in the beginning, but now we always have enough batteries. We just keep reusing the same ones, so we're saving money and helping the environment. When the batteries get low, we just stick them in the charger, and within fifteen minutes, they are fully charged and ready to go. It's so easy even a cyclops could do it.

Try it out! Run your Wii or computer wireless stuff the environmentally friendly way. Get rechargeable batteries.

Believe me, it's a much easier way to go green than trying to eat bottles and cans.

**RICK RIORDAN** is the author of the Percy Jackson and the Olympians series. He lives in San Antonio, which means he doesn't have to drive very far to find good Mexican food, which means he saves thousands of gallons of fossil fuel every year.

# WALK, CHILL, AND MAKE A PILE

## By Meg Rosoff

I live in England, which differs from the place I grew up (New England) in its weather, which is never quite so hot or so cold. But oil is much more expensive here, and everyone has a little of the old "Blitz mentality" left over from World War II, which means scrimping and saving. It also means keeping the thermostat a lot lower than my friends in the United States keep theirs, and turning the heat way way down at night. You might have to put on a sweater, but a lower thermostat has fantastic benefits—your skin won't be so dry, your lips won't get chapped, your hair will look glossier, and it's a great excuse to snuggle up under a pile of quilts at night and pretend to be Laura in *Little House in the Big Woods*.

Tip two? Walk more. Most car trips are for journeys under

a mile, so next time you're about to jump in the car, jump on your bike or walk instead. It burns calories and builds muscle, and you'll feel better about the environment, too.

My final tip is to make a compost heap! Put all the vegetable waste you create in the kitchen into a pile; add torn-up newspapers, grass clippings, leaves, etc.; and put it all into a plastic compost container, or a slatted wood box, or just a heap at the back of your yard. You're supposed to pee on it occasionally to make it really good, but I have to admit I leave that to the boys. The first time we dug the compost out of the bottom of our box, my husband was confused—"Hey," he said, "someone must have put a whole lot of good soil in here!" Duh. That's the compost, sweetheart. Black and rich and full of nutrients, it'll make your plants grow strong and healthy. Which means they fight off pests better. Which means you don't need pesticides. Which is all good news for the world.

**MEG ROSOFF** is the author of *How I Live Now*, which won the Michael L. Printz Award and the *Guardian* Award for Children's Fiction; *Just in Case*, which won the Carnegie Medal; and *What I Was*.

# A BRIGHT IDEA

## By April Halprin Wayland

Not everyone can do this, I know. So I'm not sure if I should tell you about it. But I will, in case you are one of the some-ones who can help. Or in case you're able to inspire a nearby adult to get off the couch and do it.

This summer, my husband and I sat down to figure out the cost. Ack! It was a lot. Then Gary looked at me and said, "If we don't do this, who will?"

What did we do? We put a solar roof on our house. It's in-visible from the street. You have to climb up to the roof, which I did when the solar guys were there with their ladders propped up against the side of our house.

There are twenty-eight solar electric panels. They look like those circuit boards inside computers but are made of black glass, and they are huge. Together they're nearly forty-five feet long and fifteen feet wide.

Every morning, Gary watches the electric meter on the side of our house run backward. He looks so happy! Instead of using up electricity, our house creates electricity! The electric company pays us for the power we produce. It's like we're sun farmers and our crop is energy.

Yes, it was expensive, but it lowered our electric bill big-time. What was generally two hundred dollars a month is now ninety-five cents.

There are two hurdles to putting up a solar roof.

1. You have to own the building.
2. It's expensive. But the more people buy solar roofs, the more the price will go down.

Tell your family about solar roofs. Tell your apartment owner. Tell anyone you know who owns a building. When I was young, our job was to bug adults to quit smoking. Your job is *bigger*. Our world needs you to be a solar cheerleader. Rah! Rah! Rah!

On your mark, get set, go solar!

**APRIL HALPRIN WAYLAND** is the author of *It's Not My Turn to Look for Grandma!*, *Girl Coming in for a Landing*, and *New Year at the Pier: A Rosh Hashanah Story*. When she is not printing her manuscripts on the other side of business papers, she's watching her husband watch their electric meter spin backward.

## WHAT YOU CAN DO!

Think of other ways you can use solar energy instead of electricity. On a bright sunny day, do your homework outside instead of at your desk by a lamp. Have family picnics when the weather's nice instead of eating dinner at the dining room table or in front of the TV.

# SMALL CHOICES, BIG RESULTS

## By Andrew Clements

When my wife and I and our four boys moved to Massachusetts about twenty years ago, we learned that there was no regular trash pickup in our town. Instead there was a town transfer station—a dump—and every family was responsible for getting its own trash there. So every few weeks when the barrels in the garage were full, we'd load up our minivan on a Saturday morning, and off to the dump we'd go.

Even twenty years ago, our town was working to help preserve the environment. Leaves and yard waste had to be hauled to the dump for composting—no burning allowed. And the company that runs the dump operation has been innovative about recycling glass, plastics, cardboard, and metals for all the years we've lived here.

To help my family be better at recycling, I tried to make it easy for everyone. Outside the door that leads to our garage, I installed a set of shelves, and each shelf holds two big plastic storage bins. There are two bins for paper, one for cardboard, one for glass, and one each for bottles, cans, and plastic jugs.

In twenty years, our family has recycled more than a hundred thousand pounds of stuff. That's more than fifty tons. And it hasn't been that hard.

In 2001, when the first hybrid cars became available, we got one—a Toyota Prius that uses both gasoline and electric power. This is the car my wife and I use for most of our driving. We still have a minivan for when we need to haul big things, but now some larger hybrid vehicles are available, so we're looking into getting one. The hybrids use so much less gas, and also have much lower emissions of greenhouse gases.

More recently, we've also been switching over to those curly-looking lightbulbs that put out just as much light as conventional ones while using far less electricity. They save money, save energy, and help save the atmosphere.

The most important thing is to begin right where you are, today, to save energy, to burn less fuel, to recycle everything you possibly can. Just the other day, I was looking for pancake syrup at the grocery store. I picked up one jug, and it was a kind of plastic that my town doesn't recycle. So I picked up another jug that was the right kind of reusable plastic, and that was the one I bought. I made a simple choice that was better for the earth. And we've also got reusable shopping bags now so we can stop using those thin, floppy plastic bags that are clogging streams and hanging from trees all over the planet.

Step by step, little by little, we can all change the way we shop, the way we use energy, the way we treat our home planet. And we need to do this, every one of us, today.

**ANDREW CLEMENTS** has been writing children's books for more than twenty years. His best-known book is the middle-grade novel *Frindle*.

# IT'S A WRAP!

## By Lurlene McDaniel

I think all gift-wrap paper should be banned. What a waste of resources. Be creative. Wrap gifts in the Sunday funny papers, or any piece of the newspaper, for that matter. A book? Wrap it in the book review pages. A gift for a cook? Wrap it in the food section. Heck, the recipients may actually see a recipe to their liking as a bonus.

If you don't get a newspaper, try old road maps, bright magazine pages, advertising circulars, your own drawings, coloring book pages, finger-painted sheets of paper, or even a child's writing pad where he's written letters of the alphabet—really cute!

I know a man who puts gifts into empty cereal boxes whenever possible, and I have a friend who makes her own gift bags from new paper lunch sacks that she decorates with glitter and a festive rubber stamp and ink pad. The choice of gift wrap is yours, so why not use what you already have? Think of it as a gift to planet Earth.

**LURLENE MCDANIEL** is the author of more than seventy young adult novels, most of them about teens coping with traumatic and life-altering situations. She lives in Chattanooga and is the mother of two grown sons.

# Six inches in the bathtub and hold the shampoo

## By Eve Bunting

When I talk to my grandchildren about how important it is that we save water and paper and electricity, they pay attention. They know, and I hope follow, the guidelines of turning off the water while you brush your teeth, taking shorter showers, using cloth instead of paper napkins when you can, turning off lights when you leave a room, etc. But they pay even more attention when I talk about how we saved these things and more when I was young. Most grandkids would roll their eyes at the words "when I was young," waiting for a sermon, but mine are immediately alert. They like to know how it was for me during World War II when I was in a boarding school in Belfast,

Northern Ireland, our city getting bombed and enemy planes overhead. I tell them how, for the war effort, we learned to save.

At night all the bathtubs in my boarding school were filled with water to prepare for possible incendiary bombs and fires. The buckets were at the ready for the bucket brigade. In the morning, so that we wouldn't waste water, we had to take our baths in that icy cold water.

My grandkids shiver. "Oh, Grandma! How awful."

I tell them how we were allowed to have only two baths a week, and if the overnight water had been used we could run only six inches of new water into the empty bath. We were permitted to shampoo our hair once a week.

"Oh, Grandma! Pee-ew!"

We saved paper, collecting newspapers for paper drives. Toilet paper was scarce, and on vacations from school, I remember helping my father cut up neat little squares of newspaper to place by the toilet. And those squares weren't there as reading material, either!

My grandkids giggle. "How ghastly, Grandma! No Charmin!"

"We saved and saved for the war effort, for our country," I tell them. "Now we have to save for our world. But so far it's okay to use toilet paper. Just don't use too much!"

**EVE BUNTING** has written more than two hundred books for young people. In 2002 the New York City Board of Education chose her as the Irish American Woman of the Year.

# WASHING DOGS AND DISHES

## By Peter Catalanotto

I like washing dishes. I know that's a little weird, but I do. I like it because unlike writing and painting, washing dishes is a job with a beginning and an end. When I start writing or painting, it can be unclear what to write or paint, and I always wonder if I'm truly finished or if there's something more I could do. But when I wash dishes, it's obvious when to start (when all the dishes are dirty) and it's obvious when I'm finished (when all the dishes are clean).

When I wash dishes I don't just let the water go down the drain. I put a large plastic bowl in the sink to catch the rinse water, and when it fills up I use that water for other things around the house. I'll water plants if the water's not too soapy. I'll wash the kitchen floor if it needs it. I'll wash the dogs if I can catch them. I'll even paint with it, if there are not crusts of bread or carrot peelings floating in it.

If I don't have any immediate use for the water, I'll pour it into a huge container and save it for when it will be useful.

What I like most about washing dishes is that I don't have to think about washing dishes. My mind is free to wander. Sometimes I imagine stories and pictures. Sometimes I think about how fresh water is going to be scarce someday if we're not more careful with it. And sometimes I think how nice it would be if my dogs simply washed themselves.

**PETER CATALANOTTO** has illustrated thirty-six books, thirteen of which he has written. Three of the books are about dogs. None is about washing dishes.

## WHAT YOU CAN DO!

When it's your night to do dish duty, keep the water turned off until it's time to rinse. Use a large basin to catch the water you use. Then take the dirty water you've collected and use it somewhere else!

# ALL WET

## By Bruce Hale

Who knew? All that time I thought I was enduring cruel and unusual punishment at Boy Scout camp, I was actually practicing water conservation. See, they made us take those "military-style" showers where you blast yourself with cold water, turn it off while you soap up, and finish with a cold rinse.

Back then I wasn't too crazy about the idea. But now I see its value. With the climate changing, less rain is falling, especially in California, where I live. And lower rainfall means lower water levels in the reservoirs and less water for the home. Something like three-quarters of all the water we use each day is used in the bathroom.

Did you know that a four-minute shower takes twenty to forty gallons of water? If you go military and turn off the shower while you soap up, you can save a lot.

Here's an even easier way to conserve: Turn off the water while you're brushing your teeth. After you wet your toothbrush, there's no need to leave the tap running while you're scrubbing the gunk off your teeth. You could save three gallons a day just by getting your family to follow this practice.

And finally, if you want to conserve water, flush the toilet only when really necessary. Yeah, I know—it's gross. But every time a toilet flushes, that's almost two gallons down the drain. At my house, we generally follow the old rule, "If it's yellow, let it mellow; if it's brown, flush it down."

No, that's not cruel and unusual punishment. It's just a great way to save water.

**BRUCE HALE** is the author-illustrator of more than twenty books for kids, including the popular Chet Gecko Mysteries and the Underwhere graphic novel series.

# GET THE DIRT OUT!

## By Lisa Desimini

It's hard to imagine that household cleaning products can be bad for us. They kill germs and get the dirt out, right? But they can also cause rashes, allergic reactions, sinus problems, and other health issues. I started to investigate this because of my own sensitivity. I couldn't walk into a Laundromat without getting a headache and an irritated throat and nose.

I did some research and found out that most cleaning products contain petrochemicals and other chemicals that contaminate our groundwater. If they're not disposed of properly, they wind up in landfills or get incinerated and release toxins into the environment. I don't know if you've noticed, but they also create an enormous amount of lather that takes forever to wash out. I imagined all those bubbles going down our drains and into our oceans, gathering together underground, and causing the earth to have terrible indigestion.

This was a good excuse not to wash anything at all, but after a while I had to figure something out. So I started using products that have natural ingredients. And do you know what? I felt better immediately.

Here are three recipes to share with your parents:

1. All-purpose cleanser: mix a few tablespoons of baking soda in one quart of warm water.
2. Furniture polish: Add a few drops of lemon oil to a few cups of warm water in a spray bottle. Spray on a soft, damp cloth.
3. Mold cleanser: mix one part hydrogen peroxide (three percent) with two parts water in a spray bottle. Spray and leave to dry for an hour. Rinse off.

Earth can clean itself if we let it. So please keep our Earth as healthy as possible and use natural cleansers!

**LISA DESIMINI** has illustrated more than thirty books for children, nine of which she has also written, including *My House* and *Trick-or-Treat, Smell My Feet!*

## WHAT YOU CAN DO!

Tell your parents that natural cleaning products will keep Earth its cleanest and healthiest—just like they want you to be!

# FROM REVERENCE TO RECYCLING

## By Pamela Jane

The Egyptians worshipped cats, and we adore our fluffy Ragdoll, Mittens, even though he isn't the brightest cat on the block. But as much as we love him, does he merit a fresh plastic bag for every poop? Even a pharaoh wouldn't demand that. Yet we use hundreds of plastic bags every year to clean out Mittens's litter box.

Somehow people managed in the "old days" before the ubiquitous plastic bag, and we can, too. As of today, we're switching to paper bags or waxed paper to dispose of Mittens's leavings. We'll be helping the planet, and Mittens will never know the difference!

**PAMELA JANE** has published more than twenty books for children from preschool to middle grade. She is currently working on a young adult novel.

# BIRTHDAY GREED

## By Kathleen Krull

In my book *It's My Earth, Too: How I Can Help the Earth Stay Alive*, I tell readers, "I try not to be too greedy when it's time for my birthday. People should have what they need. If they have too much, it wastes the Earth's energy."

To be human is to be greedy. It just happens. But shouldn't those of us lucky enough to live in prosperous countries try harder to get a grip on our greed?

Ever had a birthday party where people can hardly see you because of the piles of overpackaged stuff mounting up? Stuff, stuff, and more stuff? Does it ever make you feel guilty? Or even slightly ill?

Enough questions—here are a few solutions:

1. Turn your birthday party into a "Trip to the Mall with a Twist." All your friends meet at your favorite mall with the money they were going to spend on you. Everyone still gets to shop, but not for you—instead they're buying gifts that will cheer up a child who is living in a local homeless shelter.

2. Make your party a movie event. Invite friends over to watch *An Inconvenient Truth*; then discuss it afterward.

3. Ask for homemade, crafty gifts instead of store-bought items. And any birthday cards really should be handmade. Believe it or not, a handmade gift might be a treasure you keep all your life. Plus, what an excellent challenge to inspire creativity! (There are plenty of books on this topic, and useful Web sites, such as www.allfreecrafts.com/kids.)

Okay, your friends can buy you a gift. But they should buy something made from recycled materials, and something that has minimal wasteful packaging. Suggest some Web sites for shopping, like www.ecoist.com, www.greatgreengoods.com, and www.greengiftguide.com.

Remember, the most meaningful present of all is a friend's time. Suggest gift cards for movie tickets or other events you can go to together.

Have a happy green birthday!

**KATHLEEN KRULL** is the noted author of many nonfiction books for young readers.

## WHAT YOU CAN DO!

Test your creativity! What gifts can you make out of items in your house? Can you collect your favorite comics from the newspaper and use the pages to wrap your gift instead of buying expensive paper?

# FREE YOUR INNER ARTIST (START WITH SPAGHETTI)

## By James Howe

In my house, we use the mason jars that our favorite brand of spaghetti sauce comes in as drinking glasses. They're a great size and shape, and people always comment on them. (Sometimes they say, "What's up with these jars?" But mostly they think they're cool and that we're kind of cool for thinking of using them that way.) Those jars got me thinking about all the ways we can reuse the jars and other containers that stuff comes in. Just a few ideas: for holding pens and pencils, paper clips, art supplies, collections of coins or bottle caps or buttons. We can fancy them up by cutting up old magazines, newspapers, pictures, postcards, greeting cards, etc., and decoupaging the containers to make candle holders, jewelry boxes, or gift tins for candies or homemade cookies. The possibilities are endless. Instead of throwing things out (or even recycling them), bring your imagination to the idea of reusing and free your inner artist! What can you use to make jewelry? Treasure boxes? Pieces of art? Picture frames? What can you make that I'm not including?

When my daughter was younger, we did many art projects together. Collage was one of our favorite things to do, and I still have several of our collages hanging on my office walls. I also have the two glasses she decoupaged on my desk to hold my pens and pencils.

Suggest to your family that you meet once a month and brainstorm creative ways to reuse the items you would normally toss out or recycle. Find a spot in your home to turn into an arts and crafts center (it could be nothing more than a table in a corner) where you can store these items and make something new from them—together.

So what do you do after you've turned all the spaghetti sauce jars you can into drinking glasses and pencil holders? Stop buying the sauce and learn how to make your own. Cooking is another way to free your inner artist!

**JAMES HOWE** is the author of more than eighty books for young people, including the popular Bunnicula and Pinky and Rex series and *The Misfits*, the book that inspired national No Name-Calling Week. He lives in New York State.

# ALTERNATIVE POWER ROCKS

## By Shannon Hale

Here's a little secret about me—I love alternative power. Love it. I wish alternative power were a box of chocolates so I could sit with my feet up and savor every bit. I wish alternative power were a really awesome cat I could pet and snuggle. 'Kay, maybe I'm taking this metaphor thing a bit too far, but alternative power still rocks.

In our family, here are some ways we fight the filthy, nasty fossil-fuel demons and support the plight of that rock star alternative power:

1. We own a hybrid car! And we get about fifty-five miles to the gallon. My dad's car gets seventeen miles to the gallon—sucker.

2. We buy wind power. It costs a little more each month for our electricity bill, but I think it's so worth it. Just imagine, every time we turn on a light switch, instead of tapping into a smoke-spouting coal plant somewhere, we're using power generated by those tall, sleek windmills. I love wind.

3. We avoid those tempting little light switches whenever possible. We made it a priority to buy a house with lots of windows and use light-penetrable blinds, so our house is filled with sunlight! And at night we're careful to turn on only the lights we really need at the moment. Our house and furnace are also energy-efficient, as are our lightbulbs.

And we always brainstorm ways we can do more. The advances on solar panel technology are very cool, and soon you'll know our house by its roof covered in solar panels. We could drive less, live in walkable communities, carpool, just use our brains. Take that, filthy, nasty fossil-fuel demons!

**SHANNON HALE** is the author of five award-winning young adult novels, including the bestselling Newbery Honor Book *Princess Academy*. She and her husband are cowriting a series of graphic novels. They live with their two small children in Salt Lake City.

# BE A SUN SCOUT!

## By Phyllis Reynolds Naylor

Here is something so simple that anyone can do it. When the weather is cold and the sun is shining, open the blinds or curtains on the side of your house or apartment where the light comes in. Let the sun help warm your house. Don't forget that in the afternoon when the sun comes through the windows on the other side of your house, you need to open the blinds and curtains over there. Each time you do this, you are helping to save electricity or gas or oil, whichever heats your home.

When the weather is hot and you want your house to stay cool, close the blinds or curtains on the side of the house where the sun shines in. Each time you do this, you are making your house cooler and saving electricity if you have air-conditioning.

Busy moms and dads and aunts and uncles can't always pay attention to what the sun is doing. But they will thank you when they see that letting the sun be your helper can lower their fuel bills. And on a cold winter morning, a cat will thank you, too, when it is stretched out in a warm sunny spot on the rug.

**PHYLLIS REYNOLDS NAYLOR** is the author of more than 125 books, including the Newbery Award–winning *Shiloh* and the other two books in the Shiloh trilogy, *Shiloh Season* and *Saving Shiloh*. She and her husband live in Bethesda, Maryland. They are the parents of two grown sons and have three grand-children.

# PART TWO
# YOUR SCHOOL

## DID YOU KNOW?

• Almost half of all school waste comes from paper products. The average school throws away more than eight million sheets of paper per year, which adds up to almost 650 trees.

• The average student in the United States throws away sixty-seven pounds of packaging a year, including plastic water bottles, sandwich bags, molded food containers, and juice boxes.

• If everyone in the United States used one less napkin per day, we'd save a stack of napkins large enough to fill the Empire State Building and eliminate more than a billion pounds of waste each year.

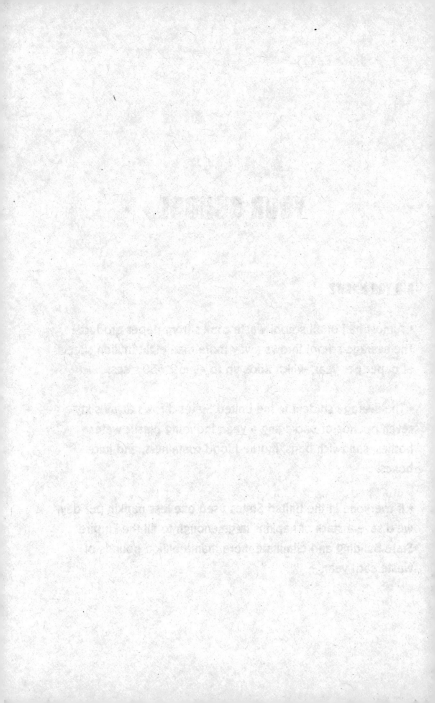

# Talking trash

## By Dana Reinhardt

How much junk is in your lunch?

And by junk I don't mean snack foods that are bad for your body. We'll talk about that important issue another time, in another book. For now I'm talking about the stuff in your lunch that you have to throw away.

I'm talking trash.

How many pieces of tinfoil or plastic wrap, or how many Ziploc bags are in your lunch box? See, I'm going to assume you carry a lunch box to school every day. Because if you don't, you can add that brown paper bag to the list of trash you generate every time the lunch bell rings.

Okay, so maybe lunch boxes aren't cool once you're in the

sixth grade. But what about a reusable insulated lunch bag? They come in plain colors. You don't have to bring Dora the Explorer or My Little Pony with you to school.

To be clear, I'm not a lunch taker, I'm a lunch packer, and it took me until this year, when I had to pack two lunches each morning, to start noticing all the unnecessary trash. Instead of just noticing it, I decided I'd try to do something about it. So I ushered in the era of the Trashless Lunch. Now I pack my daughters' grapes, crackers, cashews, and dried apricots in little reusable plastic containers. I've discovered that even sandwiches, the reliable lunch staple that comes with its very own category of plastic bag, can be cut into squares and put in plastic containers with a lid.

This might sound burdensome, but trust me, it isn't. It's actually kind of fun. I don't know why. Something about fitting all those little containers into the box gives me the same kind of satisfaction I get from loading suitcases that look like they'll never fit into the trunk of our car. It's a small success each morning to get the day started.

As with every triumph, however, there's a stumbling block. In this case: the cheese stick. As you know, cheese sticks come prewrapped in plastic. And as you also probably know, kids love them. So what to do? I could unwrap them and place them in a reusable container, throwing the trash away at home rather than at school, but that feels like cheating. So until some smart company comes out with cheese sticks that aren't individually wrapped, my trashless lunches aren't totally trashless on cheese stick days.

It's not perfect, I know, but it's a start.

**DANA REINHARDT** is the author of *A Brief Chapter in My Impossible Life*, *Harmless*, and *How to Build a House*. Until it falls into the sea, she lives in Los Angeles with her husband and two lunch box–toting daughters.

## WHAT YOU CAN DO!

At the beginning of the school year, pick out a new lunch box or insulated lunch bag that you'll be happy to tote around. Then have a parent help you pack your trashless lunch each morning!

# HAVE STAGE, WILL RECYCLE

## By Diane Roberts

As soon as word spread that Ricky Raccoon was a great story-teller, I was flooded with invitations to bring him to birthday parties as the star entertainer. Kids and adults adored him, and when he scampered onstage to tell his stories and sing his songs, they exploded in laughter. It became clear we could teach valuable lessons to kids on any subject.

Ricky Raccoon is a jovial character, with brown and black fur, and he fits nicely on my puppeteer's hand. He is the perfect vehicle to use to get my messages across.

Eventually the power company called me up, needing someone to teach schoolchildren and teachers the value of saving energy and the importance of learning to recycle. When Ricky heard of our new gig, he became interested in conservation and learned many of the ways we can help save our natural resources. We both knew these appearances weren't just more birthday fun; they were a big responsibility! And we did it, working with thousands of kids a month to pass the message along.

Ricky Raccoon invites you to learn his energy song and hopes that you, too, will become aware that we need to save our Earth for the kids of tomorrow.

*I'M RICKY RACCOON—A SAVER!*
*I'M SMART AS I CAN BE.*
*I NEVER LEAVE MY TV ON—*
*I SAVE ELECTRICITY.*

*DON'T LEAVE THE DOOR WIDE OPEN*
*WHEN YOU GO OUT TO PLAY.*
*YOU MUST REMEMBER TO SHUT THAT DOOR—*
*PLEASE DO JUST WHAT I SAY.*

**[CHORUS]**

*SAVE ALL THE ENERGY THAT YOU CAN!*
*TURN OFF LIGHTS WHEN THROUGH.*
*BE MY HELPER AND MY FRIEND.*
*CAN I DEPEND ON YOU?*
*I HAVE A PLAN THAT'S WORKING,*
*AND YOU CAN BE A PART.*

*REMIND YOUR FRIENDS TO SAVE ENERGY*
*AND THAT WILL BE A START.*

*YOU CANNOT CALL ME LAZY,*
*FOR I'M ALERT, YOU SEE,*
*BECAUSE IT'S SO IMPORTANT, FOLKS,*
*TO SAVE ALL ENERGY.*

**[REPEAT CHORUS]**

*TURN DOWN YOUR HEAT TO SIXTY-EIGHT.*
*WEAR WARMER CLOTHES, I'M TOLD.*
*AND IN THE SUMMER MONTHS, TAKE CARE—*
*DON'T KEEP YOUR HOUSE SO COLD.*

**[REPEAT CHORUS]**

**DIANE ROBERTS** is the author of *Made You Look* and *Puppet Pandemonium*. She and her puppet, Ricky Raccoon, travel from school to party to electric company spreading the word about recycling and having a great time.

# THE SWAP SHOP

## By Coleen Paratore

Once upon a time in America, long before stores the size of cities and pockets full of plastic credit cards, people traded goods. Someone had something to give away that someone else wanted, so they swapped. Say maybe one guy had too much corn and another had too many fish. The first guy was sick of making corn muffins and the other was sick of making fish fries, so they traded and went home happy. Who knows; maybe the following week they opened a diner.

Anyway, here's a free idea for you: Open a swap shop at your school. Pick a theme, like a toy swap or a book swap or a sports swap. Set up in the cafeteria or gym. Anyone who wants to participate brings in an item, which should be clean and in good working order. (Set up a few tables where you can group items by value, and label them with signs keep it simple, like "under $5" or "about $20"). Estimate the worth of your item and place it on the corresponding-value table. When the shop opens, each person who brought an item to trade gets to choose a new item of equal value to take home. Maybe do a toy swap around the holidays; a sports swap in the spring; and a book swap before summer break. You'd be surprised how one person's junk can be another person's joy.

Happy swapping!

**COLEEN PARATORE** is the author of ten books, including *The Wedding Planner's Daughter*, *The Funeral Director's Son*, *Mack McGinn's Big Win*, and *26 Big Things Small Hands Do* (in which the letter *R* is for *Recycle*).

## WHAT YOU CAN DO!

Talk to your teacher about setting up a swap shop in your school or even just in your classroom.

# Go Green at School

## By Kenneth Oppel

If you're reading this book, chances are you're already doing a lot to reduce your ecological footprint in your own home. But what about at school? Some schools have recycling and composting programs and green energy policies, but if yours doesn't, it's time to get started. Maybe there's an eco club at your school that can spearhead the campaign to go green. Talk to your homeroom teacher or principal about the best way to go about it. You'll probably need other student volunteers to make it work, as well as the cooperation of the custodial staff.

Here are some ideas to get you started:

- Make sure there's a paper recycling bin in every class

and staff workroom. Urge the teachers to make sure all their handouts are double-sided to save paper.

• When a classroom is empty, make sure to turn off the lights.

• Cafeterias produce a lot of waste. Get your school to start a composting program so food waste goes into composting bins and not garbage cans. That way, it can be recycled as fertilizer rather than ending up in a landfill.

• You can also make sure there are recycling bins in lunchrooms for glass or plastic bottles, Tetra Paks, and any paper or cardboard packaging.

• Make posters that encourage kids to bring "waste less" lunches in reusable containers (instead of plastic wrap and aluminum foil, which can't be recycled).

• Encourage students to walk or ride bikes to school. If it's not practical, how about a carpool club, so you use as little fuel as possible?

• Urge your principal to use green energy. This means the school would purchase its electricity from a company that sells energy from wind power or hydroelectric power.

• In warm months, make sure the air-conditioning isn't on too high; in winter, make sure the school isn't overheated.

• Plant some trees around your school. Not only will they make it more beautiful, they will shade it in summer and provide a windbreak in winter.

Some of these suggestions are small and easy, while others

are big and challenging. But remember that anything you do is a huge achievement.

**KENNETH OPPEL** is the author of *Silverwing*, *Airborn*, and, most recently, *Darkwing*. He lives in Toronto.

## WHAT YOU CAN DO!

Speak up and spread the world! Now that you know a little (or a lot) about helping to save the environment, it's your job to pass the information along and encourage your classmates to go green!

# A VOTE FOR THE ENVIRONMENT

## By Jennifer Armstrong

When politicians are running for office, they talk a lot about all the environmental protection laws they plan to pass. They say they're going to punish polluters, force car companies to build cars that are more energy-efficient, promote public transportation, give homeowners tax breaks if they add solar panels to their houses, put threatened animals on the endangered-species list—all kinds of things like that.

But how do we know they'll really do it once they get elected? There are lots of organizations out there that are working to protect the environment, and they keep a watchful eye on politicians. They examine the voting record of politicians in office who want to be reelected. They look at candidates' histories on environmental issues and give their opinion about how green those politicians are. Then they provide that information to the public.

You can go to the Web sites of organizations such as the Sierra Club (www.sierraclub.org), Greenpeace (www.greenpeace.org), the Federation of State Public Interest Research Groups (www.uspirg.org), and the Natural Resources Defense Council (www.nrdc.org) and learn how the candidates stack up. Take advantage of their research on the candidates, and—this is the important part—tell your parents whom to vote for! That's right! You did the research. Get your parents to vote green!

**JENNIFER ARMSTRONG** has been writing books for children and teens for more than twenty years. She lives in Saratoga Springs, New York, with her daughter.

## WHAT YOU CAN DO!

It's never too early to learn about the politicians being voted into office. Ask your social studies teacher to hold a mock election in which your class researches and debates the candidates' positions on environmental issues, then votes.

# BECOME A SCIENTIST!

## By Vicki Cobb

Five hundred years ago, people believed the sun and other planets revolved around the earth. That made sense, right? They saw the sun move across the sky every day. They saw the moon and stars rise and set. Clearly, the earth was the center of the universe.

Then one day, Galileo Galilei pointed his telescope at Jupiter and saw four moons revolving around that planet. That moment changed the world forever.

Galileo is the father of modern science, which is now a huge body of knowledge. Every belief or assumption we make can be challenged and proven right or wrong by experimentation. Today's laboratories are full of instruments vastly more sophisticated than Galileo's telescope, but in principle they are no different. They are tools that extend the human senses so that we can more fully understand the workings of the natural world.

Our life is affected every day by scientic research on health and the environment. Science will provide more and more understanding of the consequences of how we treat the planet, how we pollute it, how we destroy habitats of other living things, and how we use the planet's resources to serve our own needs. It is just becoming clear to what extent we are fouling our own nest. The solutions to the problems we have created will also come partly from science. If you do not understand how science works, you will not be able to judge the wisest courses to pursue to save the planet.

Scientists have measured the amount of carbon dioxide in the atmosphere over the past few decades and found that it is increasing. Carbon dioxide retains heat. There has always been a small amount of carbon dioxide in the air, but scientists believe that the increase is causing global warming. Virtually all scientists agree that this is happening. What causes this increase? Is it human activity, such as burning fossil fuels or destroying the rain forests? The evidence is pointing in that direction. We need to act, and quickly.

Studying science is not easy. It requires time and effort. But understanding science will keep you informed about ways you can help make a difference to the future of the earth. And you just might discover why scientists love science: because making discoveries is the best kind of fun.

**VICKI COBB** has written extensively about science for kids in books such as *Science Experiments You Can Eat*, *I Face the Wind*, and *Bet You Can't! Science Impossibilities to Fool You*.

## WHAT YOU CAN DO!

Ask your science teacher to prepare a unit on climate change and the effects of global warming on Earth's environment. At the end of the unit, get your class to band together to adopt a cause—plant a tree near the school, adopt a manatee, or hold a school cleanup day where everyone participates to make your school, and your community, a greener place to learn!

# Try to Teach Others

## By Laurence Pringle

Many people are not well informed about climate change. Some have been misled. They may have read or heard that Earth's climate is not changing or that if it is, human use of fossil fuels is not a main cause. Misinformation like this is still being spread. It's no wonder why—think of the huge industries that might suffer if people use less oil, gasoline, and coal. Some businesses have put great effort into confusing the public, trying to delay change. But armed with good information, you can clear up some confusion about this vital issue. Here are some examples:

Myth: Someone says, "Brrrr! It's cold! The temperature has been below normal for a week now. There's no global warming."

Fact: That person is talking about weather, not climate. A spell of cold weather here or there tells us nothing about Earth's overall climate. It is warming. Glaciers and Arctic ice are melting, sea levels are rising, and winters are becoming shorter.

Myth: Another person might say, "Earth's climate has changed in the past. This is just part of a natural cycle."

Fact: This is only half true. The world has indeed gone through great climate changes in the past. About eighteen thousand years ago, vast ice sheets covered much of North America and northern Europe. However, research shows that today's rapid climate change is mostly the result of human activities, especially the burning of oil and other fossil fuels.

Myth: You might hear, "Carbon dioxide isn't a pollutant. It's in our breath! And there isn't enough of it in the atmosphere to make a difference."

Fact: Again, this is half true. Yes, we exhale this gas, and all carbon dioxide is just a tiny fraction of the gases that make up Earth's atmosphere. However, carbon dioxide has a remarkable ability to trap heat in the atmosphere. When people cut and burn forests, and especially when they burn coal and other fossil fuels, they add carbon dioxide to the atmosphere. Two centuries ago 270 molecules out of every million in Earth's atmosphere were carbon dioxide. Now that number is 380 parts per million and is increasing rapidly.

Myth: Someone might say, "I heard a meteorologist at a

university say that the other scientists are all wrong. He says that the climate will soon cool."

Fact: The opinion of a university meteorologist may sound impressive. But remember, meteorology is the study of weather, not climate. Beware of "experts" who may not understand the research findings in another area of science. A few scientists deny that the atmosphere is warming because of human activity. However, their ideas have been proven wrong by the results of actual research conducted by climate scientists. Thousands of climate scientists all over the world work on the complex subject of the changing climate. They often debate about details, but they agree that humans are causing Earth's temperature to rise.

We are facing a huge challenge: to halt the climate change we are causing, thereby preventing any more harm to life on Earth. You can help by teaching others—young and old—about the science of climate change.

**LAURENCE PRINGLE** is the author of *Global Warming: The Threat of Earth's Changing Climate* and more than a hundred other nonfiction books for young adults. His books have earned numerous awards, and in 2005 he won a lifetime achievement award from the Association for the Advancement of Science.

## WHAT YOU CAN DO!

Become aware of the dangers threatening the environment and then pass that knowledge along. Is there a green committee in your school to educate students, teachers, and parents? If not, why don't you start one!

# WE'RE HISTORY . . .

## By Michael Dooling

We're history if we don't take care of our environment. Thinking green is not a new idea. The Founding Fathers of our country had some very "green" ideas about our environment. Benjamin Franklin and Thomas Jefferson were among the first American environmentalists.

In 1739 Franklin and his neighbors petitioned the Pennsylvania Assembly to stop waste dumping.

During the 1760s Franklin led a Philadelphia committee organized to help regulate waste disposal and water pollution levels.

Thomas Jefferson wrote in 1800, "The greatest service which can be rendered any country is to add an useful plant to its culture."

In 1806 Jefferson wrote, "We must use a good deal of economy in our wood, never cutting down new, where we can make the old do."

Just like Franklin and Jefferson, you can protect your environment. Pick up your trash, don't pollute the water, plant a tree, and recycle.

**MICHAEL DOOLING** is stuck in the seventies (the 1770s). He illustrates and writes books about history, including biographies of George Washington, Thomas Jefferson, and Benjamin Franklin.

## WHAT YOU CAN DO!

Learn about environmental efforts in the past twenty years—initiatives and effects. And if a particular initiative didn't succeed even though it looks like a great idea, see if you can talk your friends, teachers, parents, or state representative into taking a second look!

# THE GREEN CLASSROOM

## By Mabel and Jack Gantos

To begin a recycling program in your classroom, you first have to convince your teacher that it is important to do so. Once your teacher agrees, then you have to explain *reducing*, *reusing*, and *recycling* to the teacher and other students. These are the three Rs for turning your class into a "green class."

Reduce: Reduce the amount of paper you waste by using both sides. Reduce the amount of water you use by turning off the tap between washing items. Don't let the faucets drip. Make sure the toilet is not running. Make sure you turn off the lights when you leave the room. Don't leave radios and televisions on when you are not listening or watching. When you leave your house, make sure the heating or air-conditioning is turned down to use the smallest possible amount of energy.

Ride your bike or walk to do your errands instead of using a car. Carpool with other kids to get to school or activities.

Reuse: Try to reuse your paper cups instead of using a new one each time. A better idea is to buy a plastic water bottle that you can refill from the tap. Paper towels can be dried and reused—or use cloth rags that can be washed and used over and over. Paper bags can be reused. Clothes should be handed down instead of thrown away. Use metal utensils at lunch instead of plastic. And there are many other things you can reuse when you choose not to buy disposable products.

Recycle: Set up bins in your classroom and around school for recycling bottles, cans, and paper. If your school does not have a company that picks up recycled material, then find volunteers who will take it home to be picked up by your town. If the town does not pick up from homes, then find an adult volunteer to drive everything over to the closest recycling center.

Every kid in the classroom can help out, and once you get your classroom set up as a good example of a "green classroom," then you can win over another teacher, and another, until your entire school is green.

**JACK GANTOS** is the author of the Rotten Ralph, Joey Pigza, and Jack Henry books. **MABEL GANTOS** is a fifth grader and the superhero Reducing Girl, who wears a red costume with a big *R* on the front and zips around her school making sure students and teachers "reduce their use." The Gantoses live in Boston.

# PAPER SAVER

## By Sarah Mlynowski

I try to follow the "reduce, reuse, recycle" motto. Especially when it comes to paper. I avoid printing when I can—I write e-mails instead of letters, send e-vites instead of invitations, pay bills online. But sometimes I *really* need to see the words in print. So I decrease the margin size and the extra line spacing and make the type itty-bitty. More words on one page, fewer pages to waste, right? And then I turn to part two: reuse. As in reuse paper by printing on the other side. As for recycling, well, my blue bin is always overflowing with those double-sided messy first drafts I'm oh so relieved no one else will ever get to see.

**SARAH MLYNOWSKI** is the author of *Bras & Broomsticks*, *Frogs & French Kisses*, and *Spells & Sleeping Bags*.

## WHAT YOU CAN DO!

Be sure your classroom has a "reuse" bin for paper. Any scrap paper or worksheets that have been printed on only one side can be placed in this bin and reused for taking notes, drawing, and writing down your own ideas to save the world!

# GIANT ROBOTS—THEY'RE ALIVE!

## By Jim Paillot

Old irons; microwave oven guts; bent eggbeaters; old radio dials; rusty nuts, bolts, and screws—that stuff is like gold to my kids and me. When an old appliance finally beeps its last beep or catapults its last piece of toast, we don't just throw it in the garbage. It now has a whole new purpose. Like mad scientists, we start dissecting, disassembling, and removing all the parts that look usable and interesting. Then we recycle the remaining pieces.

Here's what happens next. We use all the cool-looking pieces and parts to make robots, birdhouses, garden sculptures, and odd-looking mechanical whatnots. Anything goes. The bodies of robots can be made from tin cans, bottles, old wood, or anything else you would otherwise throw away. The pieces can be glued together, tied with wire, or just stacked. Luckily for us, our secret Dr. Frankenstein laboratory (the garage) is loaded with lots of stuff we have saved and salvaged from other broken machines. So we seem to always have plenty of gizmos and gadgets on hand to help create our mechanical characters. Your final junk masterpiece can be painted or left as is so that your still-working appliances can turn green with envy. But don't tease your working appliances, because they still have a job to do.

As a mad scientist, you'll be helping to make the world a better, more fun place to live by creating art instead of creating bigger landfills.

And remember—the robots we create must be used for good, not evil.

**JIM PAILLOT** has illustrated many books, including Dan Gutman's My Weird School series. He lives in Arizona with his wife and their two children.

## WHAT YOU CAN DO!

Organize a creativity fair at your school in which all the entries have to be made entirely from recycled materials.

# SAVING GAS

## By Lois Duncan

It never ceases to amaze me when I see parking lots at high schools crammed with student vehicles. Surely it isn't necessary for teenagers to drive to school every day, each in his or her own car. What about taking the school bus—those big yellow things with lots of seats? Using public transportation? Riding a bicycle, which would also provide much-needed exercise after sitting in class all day? Or, at the very least, carpooling? Think of the gas that would save, and also the money!

**LOIS DUNCAN** is the author of *I Know What You Did Last Summer, Who Killed My Daughter?, Don't Look Behind You,* and many other books for young adults.

# SWAP, SHARE, SAVE

## By Kay Winters

Adults have done a pathetic job of saving our planet. Trash spills over into our streets and waterways. Abandoned cars rust in graveyards. The world grows warmer. Our water is drying up. Trees are cut down to make way for malls. Traffic clogs roadways. Every year we all use more electricity, more oil, more gas.

*More, more, more,* urge ads in the media. We are riding a roller coaster without any brakes.

What to do? Who can make a difference? You can. You can *do something* right now.

Start a swap shop club in your school. Ask a teacher to serve as adviser. Have everyone in school bring items in good condition that they'd like to swap. The PTA might help with sorting and organizing. Once a month hold a swap shop in the cafeteria, the gym, or wherever. Your club can advertise in the school and local paper, make posters for the hallway, create commercials to announce the event, and remind participants to bring their items. Make it cool to shop at the swap shop, where jackets, jewelry, boots, skateboards, board games, scooters, books, puzzles, video games, and music wait for new owners.

Will you charge money and donate the proceeds to the benefit of your school?

How many items can each student take?

Will there be a mix of items, or just sporting goods, jackets, books, games? Maybe there will be a different theme each swap shop day.

This is all up to you and your school to decide. But remember that creating something new from something old is one way to make a difference. Don't wait for adults to take action. You can do something!

Swap. Share and save. Try it.

**KAY WINTERS** was a teacher whose students used to run a book swap. Once she and her class stocked six libraries in schools on the island of Antigua. Now she is the author of *My Teacher for President*, *Abe Lincoln: The Boy Who Loved Books*, and other books for young readers.

## WHAT YOU CAN DO!

If you have items to clear out of your bedroom before a swap shop can be organized, trade with your friends! When you're finished with a bracelet, baseball glove, book, or anything else in good condition, find a friend who's ready for something new!

# PART THREE
# YOUR COMMUNITY

**DID YOU KNOW?**

• One bus can carry as many people as forty cars.

• The average U.S. citizen uses over one hundred gallons of water per day. About thirty-six states anticipate water shortages by 2016.

• Up to seventeen trees are required to make one ton of paper.

# THE SAFE WAY TO CARRY ON

## Norma Fox Mazer

I am seriously worried about the air we breathe, the water we drink, and the soil that grows our food. In short, I'm seriously worried about the world we live in and what's happening to it. A few years ago, our local supermarket began accepting plastic bags for recycling. Plastic bags compress amazingly well, and every few weeks, I would dump a fresh clump of them into the recycle bin. And walk away, smugly virtuous, convinced I was doing my bit to save the environment.

Well, it was a good thing to do, no doubt about that. Still, I grew uneasy about the sheer number of bags I was accumulating and recycling. Plastic bags—and not just mine—seemed as endless as grains of sand on the beach. I started reusing mine around the house to line wastebaskets and to cover food in the refrigerator. Recently, though, I read an alarming statistic about the oil needed to make these bags and the evil ways they can harm the environment, especially the ocean, where whales, dolphins, seals, and sea turtles mistake the plastic for food, eat it, and die.

I've made a New Year's resolution to break the plastic bag habit. To do away entirely with plastic bags in my life. After all, I grew up without plastic bags, as did my sisters and my parents and my aunts and my uncles. So now I never go anywhere without my backpack and cloth bags to carry whatever needs to be packed or carried. No, I lie. I still forget at times and find myself accepting plastic. I'm working on it. I intend to make the no-plastic-bag rule so ingrained that going into a store without a cloth bag or backpack will seem as dangerous as driving without a seat belt. Which it is.

**NORMA FOX MAZER** has written nearly thirty novels and short-story collections for young adults, including *Missing Pieces*, *Out of Control*, *Girlhearts*, and the Newbery Honor Book *After the Rain*.

## WHAT YOU CAN DO!

If your local supermarket doesn't sell canvas bags, ask it to start. The supermarket and other local businesses could put their logos on the bags—free advertising as they help to save the environment by minimizing the use of plastic bags.

# IN PRAISE OF FEET

## By Ann Brashares

I will tell you a strange fact about me. Though I am an adult and a mother of three, I do not have a driver's license. I can drive. I used to drive. But I don't anymore. The main reason for this is that I live in two of the few places in the world where you don't need to drive—New York City and Fire Island. In New York, I can walk almost everywhere I need to go. I love walking. And if I can't walk, I can easily take the bus or subway. On Fire Island, which is a summer beach community, cars are not allowed, so everyone walks or bikes. We pull our stuff in wagons and take our shopping home in the baskets of our bikes.

The reason I live the way I do is that I don't like cars very much. They are useful, I know. And I do take advantage of them sometimes. Our world is set up for them—they are hard to avoid. But in my ideal world, there are no cars.

So picture it. If you don't have cars, people ride bikes or walk. They live a little closer together and have tighter communities. They don't have to worry about kids getting hit by cars or drunk-driving accidents or carjacking. They don't have to worry about almost any crime—cars are what make the getaway possible. With all that exercise of walking and biking, people don't have to worry about obesity much anymore (which is getting to be the single worst national health problem). Their hearts and bodies are healthier. And imagine how much healthier the planet is. Radically reduced carbon emissions—a virtual halt to climate change. A lot less pollution. And the world looks a lot more beautiful, too. Cars, big-box stores, highways, and parking lots are just not very pretty. Also, imagine how it transforms world politics: If we don't use very much oil, the constant troubles in the Middle East get a whole lot simpler.

In my ideal world, you can walk to school, and your parents can walk or ride bikes to work. We live closer together, so you can walk or bike to the stores and parks and movie theaters. The layout of our world and the way we spend our time change. No more traffic or two-hour commutes.

In the words of John Lennon, you may say I'm a dreamer. I know, I know. But let me propose a simple thing that you and your family can easily do. Make sure everyone in your family has a working bike with a good basket. About eighty percent of the places most people go are within two miles of home—which is very easy biking distance. So if you are going less than a mile or two from home, take your bike. It's a lot more fun than piling into the car. Or you can choose one day of the week to make a No-Car Day in your family. For example, make Saturday the day you bike to your soccer game or the movie theater or your best friend's house. Even that one small thing can change the world.

**ANN BRASHARES** is the author of the *New York Times* bestselling series The Sisterhood of the Traveling Pants.

# Be a Green Detective

## by Kathleen V. Kudlinski

In my personal life, I am a careful recycler, driving my family nuts, nagging about how much garbage we create. Instead of using a garbage collection service, we drive weekly to the town dump, where there are even recycling bins for office-paper waste. As a writer, I make plenty of rough drafts so bad they should never be read again!

As a speaker at schools, conferences, and local clubs, I always remind people that every one of us needs to combat global warming. In schools I encourage kids to ask if the school office recycles paper. Does their cafeteria recycle the giant glass jars and plastic bottles they go through daily? Are there recycling bins for the plastic and glass bottles kids bring in their lunches from home? I even tell kids to peek into the teachers' lounge. If it has a soda machine, is there a recycling bin for empty cans? How about your own home? Or your parents' workplaces? Town hall? Local restaurants? Does everyone realize that making a plastic bottle of water uses up more water than the bottle contains—plus the oil to make the bottle, then truck bottles around and recycle them? A pushy kid can change the actions of everyone around him or her.

In my weekly newspaper column, I nudge everyone by presenting news about global warming—especially how it affects my readers. But adults are often more impressed by an activist kid than they are by regular old writers like me. Local newspapers are happy to publish (for free!) thoughtful "letters to the editor" by kids. Readers know about the polar bear's problems with melting ice, of course. But do they hear about the changes in their local bird population? Or the changing growing season in their own town? Or the drying up of a pond you remember from your childhood? It is easy to find startling facts on the Internet or with a quick phone call to a local agency. I tell kids to be bold—adults are extra impressed by, and helpful to, a kid with good questions!

KATHLEEN KUDLINSKI is the author of thirty-eight children's books, including science picture books, middle-grade biographies, and historical novels and young adult books. For twenty years she has written and illustrated "The Naturalist," a prizewinning Sunday column in the *New Haven Register* (Connecticut).

## WHAT YOU CAN DO!

Write to your local newspaper about the things your town can do to help save the environment. Ask your teacher to give extra credit to any student who writes a worthy letter, and see your letters published where your voices can be heard!

# And the Award Goes to . . .

## By Bonnie Bryant

Who, me? Competitive? Don't be silly. I don't like to compete. Not at all. Unless I'm pretty sure I can win. Then it's okay.

Sometimes as I drive around the town where I spend my summers, I notice how people pile their garbage and recyclables. Can you imagine anything less exciting to care about? Ah, but I get hints that way. I saw that one family has a neat double-can thing they can roll down their long driveway, so I bought a can with wheels. Another family was remodeling, and they had a lot of special-pickup items. Seeing their pile reminded me to put out my broken bed rails for special pickup that night. And another family only ever had to put out half a bag of garbage and just a little recycling. How could they have so little garbage? I live alone and I've got twice the garbage.

You're probably thinking, "Get a life, Bonnie." But like I said, I'm competitive when I want to win. One time, the pickup people had a contest where they announced they would award twenty-five dollars to the household with the neatest recycling for one week. I did everything short of ironing my newspapers back into pristine newness. The newspapers were neatly stacked and sacked, lying tidily on top of the sterilized glass, metal, and plastic (we're allowed to commingle materials), and the blue box was precisely parallel to the street. It wasn't the twenty-five dollars that motivated me. It was the glory. I mean, once you've won an award like Neatest Recycler, well, nobody can take it away from you.

When I was done, I checked out my neighbors' work. I was confident mine was the neatest on the street. Would it be enough?

The phone didn't ring. I didn't get my picture in the paper. I didn't win the twenty-five dollars. But I did learn that it was a whole lot easier to carry tidy recycling to the curb than to dribble slippery newspapers from home to street. It also made it easier for the guys to load my stuff on the recycling truck. I'm not quite as fastidious as I was that one week, but I'm much tidier than I was before. Anything we can do to facilitate recycling is a good thing, and that's a competition I'm more than willing to enter.

**BONNIE BRYANT** is the author of the Saddle Club series, which has been made into a television show aired on PBS and Discovery Kids.

# Proud to Be a Nimby

**By Iain Lawrence**

I live on an island that's known as The Rock, a lump of sand-stone covered with trees and fields and houses. It's home for nearly five thousand people, and probably just as many deer. It seemed an idyllic place, until our public utility announced plans to build a power plant on the neighboring point of land.

At first I thought it might not be a bad idea to have a power plant nearby. Our electricity goes out with nearly every winter storm. Whenever the wind picks up, so do sales of bottled water, canned food, and gasoline for generators. I went to an open house sponsored by the project's engineers and was told that there would soon be blackouts on winter nights if the power plant was not built. I was assured that there was no other place to put it and that it would run on natural gas, so that it would be clean and safe and quiet. It would even be painted green to blend in with the trees. Why, I would hardly know it was there. I believed what I was told.

But other people were not as easily convinced. A group of islanders came together to write letters and petitions to block construction of the power plant. My partner, a quilt maker, got people making protest quilts, and island artists showed their opposition by creating pictures of spoiled paradise and smoky ruin. She asked if I wanted to help, but I said no; I didn't want blackouts on winter nights.

She started showing me things people had written about power plants that run on natural gas. I saw that it's a tremendous waste of energy to pump fuel hundreds of miles, then burn it to make electricity to heat the homes next door. I saw that burning huge volumes of natural gas isn't really so safe and clean. Emissions are dangerous to people's health and bad for the planet. I learned that our public utility had already tried to build the plant twice, in different communities, only to have the plans blocked by local protests. I learned that the utility itself had tried to stop construction of a similar plant, saying the pollution would be too dangerous.

I joined the fight against the plant, in the small way that I could. I painted a square for the protest quilts. I helped with letter writing, so that the experts could explain their concerns more clearly.

Of course, there were other people who wanted the plant to be built. They criticized the protesters as "NIMBYs" fighting against a common good for the selfish principle of "Not in My Back Yard." They said the protestors wouldn't be protesting if the plant were being built a thousand miles away, or a hundred miles away, or even half a hundred miles away.

Well, that may be true, but I don't think there's anything wrong with it. There's no shame in being a NIMBY. It's only a very recent development, after all, that the average person has traveled at least fifty miles from home. Now the whole world is our backyard, and if every person protected his or her own little part of it, all of us would be that much better off.

The power plant was never built. The public utility began to look for other ways to make electricity, inviting proposals for generators run by wind and water. We still haven't had our blackouts on winter nights, and I'm proud to be a NIMBY.

**IAIN LAWRENCE** is the author of numerous acclaimed novels, including *The Cannibals*, *The Convicts*, *Gemini Summer*, *B for Buster*, *The Lightkeeper's Daughter*, *Lord of the Nutcracker Men*, and *Ghost Boy*. He lives on Gabriola Island in British Columbia, Canada.

# WHERE THE ANIMALS AND BIRDS STILL LIVE

## By Gloria Whelan

Forty years ago my husband and I discovered a little lake in the middle of the woods. As we grew to love the woods and the water, we worried that one day after we were gone the developers would come and cut down the woods and ring the lake with houses. We put a conservation easement on our property, giving the development rights to the Grand Traverse Regional Land Conservancy. That means we can sell the property or leave it to our children, but no one can ever build on it. It will always stay just as I describe it in many of my books. The herons and eagles, the hawks and kingfishers will still fly over the lake. The fox will trot around the lake,

148

the deer will drink at the lake's edge, and the bears will still go berrying where I have.

**GLORIA WHELAN** has written more than thirty-five books for young readers. Her novel *Homeless Bird* received a National Book Award.

## WHAT YOU CAN DO!

Is there an area in your town that needs to be protected against development? Talk to your teachers and community leaders about preserving areas with natural resources and wildlife.

# Stamp Out Witches' Drawers

## By Jon Scieszka

I hate plastic bags.

I hate the crinkly white ones tumbling down my street in Brooklyn.

I hate the shiny black ones lurking in the bushes in the park.

I hate the little orange ones flapping around the subway tracks.

And I've never seen it in person, but I just heard about it—a huge underwater mass of discarded plastic bags, covering an area bigger than the state of Texas, floating somewhere out in the Pacific Ocean. I hate them, too.

But the plastic bags I hate most are the ones snagged in the trees. They ride a breeze, grab a branch, and then never let go. The wind rips them. The rain splatters them. Still they don't let go. They hang there, dirty and ratty. Ugly as witches' drawers.

I don't know who first called them that. But it sounds right to me.

So whenever anyone offers me a plastic bag, I think of ratty witches' underwear and say, "No thanks."

Please do the same.

And together we can stamp out witches' drawers.

**JON SCIESZKA** is the author of *The True Story of the 3 Little Pigs!*, *The Stinky Cheese Man,* the Time Warp Trio series, the Trucktown series, and a bunch of other stuff. In 2008 he was named the first National Ambassador for Young People's Literature.

## WHAT YOU CAN DO!

Use a cloth bag when you run errands. Eliminating the use of plastic bags will reduce plastic waste and prevent the bags from littering your town.

# SHARING OUR WEALTH

## By Johanna Hurwitz

My parents taught me to recycle long before the word entered popular usage. We called it sharing. Whenever we had something in quantity or something that we weren't using ourselves, we would give it away to others. Thus all these years later I look for a new home for each book I finish reading that I don't expect to reread. (Don't worry, I have hundreds upon hundreds of books in my house.) In this way I share my pleasure in the text and also have someone to discuss it with when they are finished reading. "Feel free to give it on to someone else," I always tell my friends.

Old magazines I give to a friend who is a collage artist. She cuts them up and uses them in the most amazingly creative ways.

When an article of clothing doesn't seem to fit as well as it once did, when a pocketbook just sits in my closet unused, when a pair of shoes begins to pinch my feet, I give these items to someone who can use and enjoy them. Last year in India I bought a pair of cotton slacks made of hand-printed fabric. I fell in love with the print and so, even though the pants were slightly snug, I bought them. If I lose five pounds they should fit me just fine, I thought. Well, a year later these pants are still snug. I'm searching for the perfect home for them, and to this end I've already offered them to three different friends. But like the glass slipper that Cinderella dropped, the pants are too small. Someday I will find the friend or acquaintance for whom the pants are perfectly sized.

Every time I stay at a hotel, there are free toiletries waiting for me: little bottles of shampoo, conditioner, and body lotion, and small bars of beautifully fragranced soap. These "gifts" from the hotel are included in the cost of my stay. So I take them home and donate them to homeless shelters, where I know they will be well used.

I'm a knitter, and like all people who knit, I have loads of leftover yarn. This I divide between a friend who is teaching her students how to knit and someone else who uses these odd collections of yarn to knit or crochet caps for balding cancer patients.

When I bake a cake or make a pot of soup or a batch of applesauce, I always put some aside for elderly neighbors. I also give them any new brand of cat food that my cat refused to try. Their pets seem less fussy than mine.

So my garbage pail is almost empty. But my life is full of friends.

**JOHANNA HURWITZ**, a former librarian, writes realistic fiction, including *Mostly Monty*, *Squirrel World*, *Fourth-Grade Fuss*, *Baseball Fever*, *Class Clown*, and many other books. She lives in Great Neck, New York.

# Blowin' in the Wind

## By Margie Palatini

What's that sound we hear beginning with the earliest signs of spring and lasting until the last leaf hits the ground in autumn?

Squirrels chattering?

Birds twittering?

Bees buzzing?

Nah.

Who can hear any of that?

Not with leaf blowers and lawn mowers taking over every yard in every neighborhood.

(Are those machines really just lawn mowers? Please. They look like Transformers on steroids.) Yes, there actually was a time when "gardening" was considered a relaxing and quiet hobby.

People puttered.

That's right. Shocking, I know, but people really did putter around in their own yards.

For enjoyment. Imagine that.

A quiet clip-clip here. A clip-clip there. Flower beds. Vegetable gardens. Hedges trimmed by hand.

Days gone by. Yes, days gone by.

Today a person can't sit in his or her own backyard without wearing earplugs.

Yeah, yeah, I'm venting, and you're asking, "What does this have to do with what everyone else has been talking about?"

Only that one of those lawn mowers or leaf blowers creates about ten times more air pollution than a car. And we all know what those things are doing to this planet!

So, here's a simple thought:

Use a *rake*!

And while we're at it, how about a push mower? A plain old shovel when the snow comes a-falling? . . . Is there anything more beautiful and peaceful than newly fallen snow?

What? What? Can't hear you.

Someone is using a snowblower.

Seriously. All this unnecessary noise pollution is contributing to serious planetary air pollution.

Is it really so important not to see a stray leaf on our

lawns? For blades of grass to be mowed to a perfectly measured centimeter?

Great grass—or Greenland being swallowed into the ocean? Think about it.

**MARGIE PALATINI** is the author of more than thirty award-winning and laugh-out-loud-funny picture books, such as *Piggie Pie!*, *Bedhead*, *The Web Files*, *Bad Boys*, *Sweet Tooth*, *Three French Hens*, and *The Cheese*. She lives with her family in New Jersey, where she is slowly going deaf.

## WHAT YOU CAN DO!

Grab your rake or your shovel and offer your time to help clean up yards or public spaces around your town!

# PASSING IT ON(LINE)

## By Margo Rabb

For five years my husband and I have lived in a one-bedroom apartment. This was plenty of space until a year ago, when our daughter was born. Perhaps you haven't noticed, but babies and stuff go together. And baby stuff tends to be big. And its usefulness doesn't last long—in three months we need new things. The result: a major lack-of-storage problem. And that, combined with my hope that the planet will still be in existence for my daughter to enjoy as she grows older, has led me to a modern solution to the problem of Too Much Stuff.

I'm a devoted member of several Yahoo! groups for parents in my neighborhood, where we can post for anything we're hoping to find used or that we want to give away. I've found great used clothes, toys, and DVDs and passed plenty of clothes and toys on to others in the neighborhood. I've even gotten some great things that were never even used and still had tags on them. And it's not just baby stuff—members pass on older kids' clothes, toys, books, electronic gadgets, and basically anything that might be useful to someone else.

Now, before I buy anything new, I post on the neighborhood Yahoo! groups first, to see if anyone has the item to give away or sell cheaply. So if there's a new toy or DVD that you'd like to have, ask your parents to join the online parents' group in your neighborhood, and see if you can get what you want there first (and pass on some of your old toys at the same time). And if there isn't an online parents' group, then ask yours to start one!

**MARGO RABB** is the author of *Cures for Heartbreak*. She lives in Brooklyn, New York.

# SAVE THE TOYS!

## By Suzy Kline

Last Sunday my grandchildren, my daughter, and I took a hard look at all the toys that had accumulated in their house over the past seven years. Which ones weren't they playing with anymore? We filled *four huge boxes*! Those once-loved treasures were brought to our Open-Air Mall.

"What's that place?" you ask. "The Open-Air Mall?"

That wonderful place is at our local recycling plant (the one I used to call the dump!). If you visit yours, you may find lots of new recycling areas. Our Open-Air Mall is where you take all your "still-good stuff"!

So . . . Mr. Potato Head, a few garages and farms with Little People, jack-in-the-boxes, plush toys, fire engines, cash registers, blocks in a wagon, and a dozen stuffed animals and lots more *stuff* are all safely inside a one-room shelter just waiting to be adopted. Anyone can select a toy that's "new to you!"

The good part is that the toys are not going to be thrown out and buried in some landfill that is growing and *growing* and GROWING too fast!

The best part is that you're helping to save our planet! Saving toys is something you can do yourself with just a little help from Mom or Dad or Grandma or Grandpa.

Visit your local recycling plant this week!

**SUZY KLINE** is the author of several series featuring Horrible Harry and Herbie Jones.

## WHAT YOU CAN DO!

If your community doesn't already have an Open-Air Mall, look for places to start one. It could be at your town's recycling center, a church, a school, or even a specially organized fair that your town could host a couple of times a year.

# What's in the Bag?

## By Linda Sue Park

Every Saturday, my husband brings home a heavy brown paper bag.

We never know what's going to be in it.

Well, that's not quite true. We know it's going to be full of fruits and vegetables, but we don't know what kind. It's like getting a surprise every week.

Some Saturdays, the bag holds sugar-sweet melons. Or peppers in party colors—scarlet, gold, emerald. Or squash with nice names: Delicata, Sweet Dumpling, Ambercup. Other weeks, there might be zucchini. And more zucchini. A *lot* of zucchini.

We get this wonderful treat every week from June through November because we subscribe to a local CSA farm. CSA stands for *community supported agriculture*. Farmers who enroll in CSA agree to supply organically grown produce to subscribers, who pay a set fee and pick up one bag of produce a week. (Some CSA farms also require subscribers to work a few hours a month.)

What if you don't have easy access to a CSA farm? Most families can still buy organic food at their local stores. According to the *New York Times*, buying the local or organic version of even one of five foods helps make a difference to either human health or the environment or both. The Big Five are: milk, potatoes, peanut butter, ketchup, and apples.

And locally grown organic food tastes better. It really does! Even my kids noticed!

Are there any drawbacks? Well, maybe one or two. *Organic* means that the farmer uses fewer chemicals like pesticides, which can be harmful to both people and the planet. No pesticides—so there might be caterpillars in the broccoli. (Yuck.) We've gotten used to that, and have learned an effective de-caterpillaring technique. (Soak the broccoli head down in cold salted water for a few minutes.) And sometimes there's just too much zucchini.

**LINDA SUE PARK** is the author of several books for young people, including the Newbery Medal winner *A Single Shard*. She lives with her family outside Rochester, New York.

## WHAT YOU CAN DO!

Find out if there is a CSA project in your area by going to www.localharvest.org/csa.

# Peanuts, Anyone?

## By Sonia Levitin

I do love peanuts. I like to toss them to the elephants at the zoo. I like to pop them, chew them, crunch them, either raw or roasted, salted or plain. I bake them into brownies and toss them into my cereal and stick them together with gooey stuff to make my own cereal-nut bars.

But the kind of peanuts I'm going to talk about here are the white puffy kind used for packing. I order lots of stuff on the Internet, and I'm always amazed at the enormous box that the delivery man plunks down in my hall when all I've ordered is a small set of coffee mugs or a single bud vase. I open the box, and immediately they tumble out: peanuts. Packing peanuts. They remind me of marshmallows or pieces of cloud or small balls of cotton candy. They actually look good enough to eat, but I wouldn't try it, and I hope you won't, either. I scoop them up quickly so that my dogs won't think they are chew toys.

The question is, what do you do with all those packing peanuts?

I suppose I could collect enough of them to make a stack high enough to slide down or jump on, sort of like a haystack but totally inorganic.

I suppose, if I were in an artsy-craftsy mood, I could spray them with gold paint and glitter, to be the base for a winter arrangement of pinecones and pine branches. Or I could make a wreath of heavy cardboard and glue them on, paint them green, and add beads or holly berries. Or I could glue them onto an empty oatmeal box or any old jar and use acrylic paint to create a bright container. I would paint every peanut a different color and maybe add sequins or seashells.

But because I am usually writing or hiking with my dogs, Buddy and Shadow, or cooking up a hearty soup or stew, I do something quite different with all the peanuts that collect in my house. I shove them into a box and take them down to the local shopping center, where I present them to the owner of our small packing store. He is always delighted to have this gift, and he reuses the peanuts in packages.

The same goes for bubble wrap. Now, I know I could save it for Halloween and make a beautiful ballerina costume. I could sew a bubble-wrap shirt and cape and decorate my bubble-wrap costume with gold spray paint and glitter. But I know I won't do that, because I will save some for wrapping gifts, and the rest will go to my friend at the packing store, to be reused and end up in some undisclosed, mysterious destination. Now that I think of it, maybe I should attach a note, like a message in a bottle. . . .

**SONIA LEVITIN** is the author of more than forty books in various genres—picture books, mysteries, science fiction, and contemporary novels. Her latest books are *Junk Man's Daughter* and *Strange Relations*.

# Eat a Real Tomato, Save the Planet

## By Will Hobbs

Don't lose heart thinking about the numbers. Keep the faith. Yes, there are more than six billion people on the planet, but one individual can help put the brakes on abrupt, human-caused climate change. There are hundreds of ways you and your family can slow the consumption of fossil fuels. Here's one you may not have thought about: Buy locally produced vegetables, fruits, and meats from your local farmers' market. About thirteen percent of the foods Americans consume are produced outside our country. The lion's share is produced in this country but at a great distance from the grocery store where you shop. Think of the energy consumed by ships, trucks, trains, and even airplanes to move all that food around. Talk about contributing to global warming.

Some of you may already be growing a percentage of your own food. If you're not, do you have a space in your yard to plant a vegetable garden? Fruit trees? When my wife and I first moved to Colorado years ago, we wanted to see if we could raise most of our own food, to become as self-sustaining as possible. We had a giant vegetable garden, chickens, rabbits, and dairy goats. We are no longer able to do that, but you'll find us almost every Saturday at our local farmers' market trying to support community-based agriculture. Plus the food is so much more delicious! The tomatoes offered at most chain groceries are picked green and hard as rocks, then gassed to make them turn red. Fruit isn't allowed to stay on the tree long enough to ripen. I'm sure you can think of a lot more examples of less-than-perfect produce you've bought at the supermarket.

One of my novels, *Kokopelli's Flute*, reflects my love of gardening. The title refers to the humpbacked flute player and ancient seed carrier of America, Kokopelli. I hope you'll get a chance to read it one day, but mostly I hope you'll plant some seeds of your own. There's a lot of fun in seeing them sprout and grow, flower and come to fruition. Eat a real tomato and save the planet!

**WILL HOBBS** is the award-winning author of numerous books for young readers, including *Downriver*, *Crossing the Wire*, *Far North*, and *Go Big or Go Home*. He lives in Durango, Colorado.

# PLANTS: A MATTER OF LIFE AND BREATH

## By Pat Brisson

Everyone knows that plants supply us with the food we eat. And most everyone knows that plants also provide oxygen and humidity to the air we breathe—something we lose when areas are covered with concrete. But plants are important for other reasons, too.

The right plants can turn your yard into a home for butterflies. This is important, since houses, parking lots, and malls are replacing their natural habitats. Although butterflies frequently get nectar from many plants, they only lay their eggs on the one or two specific host plants that their caterpillars feed on.

Native plants are species that have been growing in a certain area for hundreds of years and are perfectly suited to the climate and soil of that area. They've been providing shelter and food to butterflies for all that time, so when those plants are gone, the survival of that particular butterfly is threatened.

Native plants are not always the ones with the prettiest flowers, but butterflies will think they're beautiful! Look for information on the North American Butterfly Association Web site (www.naba.org) or at www.butterflywebsite.com. Providing the plants that butterflies need to grow will give you the chance to watch—up close—all stages of their growth cycle and to better appreciate the grace and beauty of these fascinating creatures.

Did you know plants remove toxins from the air in our homes, schools, and businesses? Carpets, draperies, synthetic materials, computers, copy machines, building materials, cleaning chemicals, and even people put toxins into the air we breathe. Household plants can remove those toxins and provide oxygen and humidity. Plants are also beautiful, help people feel good by bringing them closer to nature, and reduce the amount of mold and bacteria in their vicinity.

So add some plants to your life, both indoors and out. You'll breathe easier, surround yourself with beauty, and be able to take satisfaction in knowing you're giving butterflies a chance to keep on living.

**PAT BRISSON** has written eighteen books for young people and enjoys meeting her readers on author visits to schools. She tends her butterfly garden in Phillipsburg, New Jersey.

## WHAT YOU CAN DO!

Ask your teacher or a community leader to help you organize a fund-raiser to sell plants for a holiday like Mother's Day. It's an easy way for you to get a gift and it's good for the environment! You can even use the proceeds to plant more trees in your town.

# EARTH ANGELS

## By Tanya Lee Stone

Several years ago, I was in the grocery store, and a clerk was pulling all kinds of fresh food off the shelves and loading it up in a cart. "What are you doing?" I asked.

"This stuff has yesterday's expiration date on it, so I can't sell it anymore," she said.

"What do you do with the food?" I asked.

"Oh, we just throw it in the Dumpster."

I couldn't believe it. One minute earlier, it was the same food I would have taken off the shelf and purchased. And here's the truth about expiration dates: Most of the time, food is good for four to five days after the sell-by date stamped on a container. There was absolutely nothing wrong with the

172

mountain of food that was about to go into the Dumpster. Beautiful fruits and vegetables, cheese, yogurt, milk, roasted chickens—the works. I couldn't get the image out of my head. In most towns and cities, there are people who have trouble affording enough healthy food to eat, and here was just one grocery store throwing out enough fresh food to feed fifty people that day. Well, I got right to work.

I called all the grocery stores, restaurants, and caterers in my city to find out who else had this problem of expired food to deal with. I also called all my friends and started a volunteer network on the spot. By the end of the week, we were picking up food and driving it to the food shelf and the other shelters that serve food to people in need. I called our effort Project Angel Food. Within a few months, we were transporting five hundred pounds of fresh food a week to nonprofit groups in the area.

People asked me how I managed to do something as complicated as starting my own nonprofit, putting together a volunteer network, and delivering so much food each week, all while taking care of my children and writing books. But here's my big secret—it wasn't complicated at all.

Some things just sound hard. But if you simply roll up your sleeves and decide to get it done, it's as easy as walking—left foot, right foot. One step at a time.

Look around. Do you see a problem you want to solve? You have that power. Earn your wings. Be an Earth Angel. It will make you feel so good, you'll think you can fly!

**TANYA LEE STONE** has written more than eighty books for kids, including the young adult novel *A Bad Boy Can Be Good for a Girl* and picture books such as *Elizabeth Leads the Way* and *Sandy's Circus*.

## WHAT YOU CAN DO!

Is there a grocery store, food pantry, or shelter in or near your town? Ask your parents to help you organize food donations. Don't let good food go to waste if you can give it to those in need!

# Found Objects

## By Susan Patron

In my book *The Higher Power of Lucky*, the main character, Lucky, has a job at the Found Object Wind Chime Museum and Visitor Center in the tiny desert town of Hard Pan, California. Why a museum of wind chimes made from found objects? I wanted to show how people of very limited resources can come together as a community in which, despite poverty and loss and huge challenges, people reclaim things that have been abandoned and then recycle them as useful or beautiful objects. Lucky learns to look beyond the old shacks and sheds and rusted cars to see beauty in the place where she lives.

Here are some examples of things that many people would see as trash: old tin cans, discarded lengths of phone wire, shards of broken pottery and glass, cherry pits, scraps of worn fabric that are too small to be of use.

Useless junk? Well, wait. Maybe we can reclaim this rubbish if we learn to look at it through the eyes of the artists and inventors who transform someone's trash into something else altogether:

- In the ghost town of Bodie, California, flattened tin cans, their tops and bottoms removed, cover the outer walls of a small home. The neatly overlapping rusted tin rectangles create a beautiful effect, like scales on a fish.

- Zulu artisans of South Africa craft baskets from discarded phone wire, weaving different colors together to create intricate, swirling patterns.

- At Watts Towers in Los Angeles, interconnected constructions made from scrap rebar and mortar are inlaid with pieces of porcelain, tile, seashells, and glass.

- Cherry pits can be heated and hold heat for a long time. PK, a character in my book *Maybe Yes, Maybe No, Maybe Maybe*, collects cherry pits because she knows they will make an excellent foot warmer if sewn into a small cloth bag.

- Years before I was born, my grandmother made a quilt out of pieces of fabric salvaged from the worn-out dresses and shirts of her ten children. The quilt is now on my bed, so I am warmed by my mom and aunts and uncles, and by a grandmother I hardly knew.

**Susan Patron** is the author of six books for children, including the Newbery Medal–winning book *The Higher Power of Lucky*.

## WHAT YOU CAN DO!

Before you throw something away, think about the other uses it may have. Is there a donation center in your town that will collect old toys, clothes, or furniture? Do you know any budding artists who make eccentric creations? What if you saved all the money you get from recycling cans and bottles for a year? Saving items from the trash can add up to saving the world!

# GREENKID

## By Rosemary Wells

My daughter, Marguerite, was born laughing and born green. She was raised in a very conventional suburb of New York City. But she was different from the other kids. She always spent her time after school in the woods, learning the names of all the trees and animals. Later she went on to Tom Brown Jr.'s Tracker School to learn about outdoor survival. I was terrified that she would be done in by the pinelands of New Jersey with no matches, fire, or food. But she survived Tom Brown style and went on to study animal science at Cornell University. Now she is an organic farmer in Ithaca, New York, and runs Cornell's organic research farm part-time. She owns a truck and a car and never buys gas or stops in a gas station. She uses only cooking oil to fuel them and pays almost nothing to drive three hundred miles, because all her fuel is free at the local hamburger restaurant. The cost of converting a car's motor to burn cooking oil is quickly paid for by the money she saves on gasoline. Not only would we improve our Earth's air immeasurably if we all ran our cars on cooking oil, we'd save money and not be dependent on foreign oil. And we wouldn't have to worry about drilling for oil in Alaska and ruining a beautiful natural habitat just so we can drive to the mall.

**ROSEMARY WELLS** is the author and illustrator of more than a hundred books for young readers.

# You don't need a pedigree to purr

## By Susan Beth Pfeffer

Clarence Darrow, perhaps the best-known lawyer in twentieth-century America, was renowned for his support of liberal causes. But when asked to show his support for birth control, he declined, explaining that he was the fifth of eight children, and it would be hypocritical of him to urge others to have small families. After all, if his parents had done so, he wouldn't exist.

I feel somewhat the same way about urging people to recycle, recycle, recycle. My livelihood is dependent on people buying my latest product—my newest book. So how can I say, "Don't buy gift-wrap paper; use newspapers instead," when someone else's livelihood is dependent on the purchase of brand-new, shiny, pretty gift-wrap paper?

What I can in good conscience suggest is that people get their pets from animal shelters. Just about every cat I've ever had started out as an animal shelter kitten. They're every bit as cute, affectionate, and demanding as expensive store-bought cats. Because my cats have been spayed or neutered, they'll never bring unwanted litters of kittens into the world. As long as Clarence Darrow doesn't hear about it, I can publicly endorse birth control for cats!

**SUSAN BETH PFEFFER** is the author of more than seventy books for children and young adults. Her most recent book, *The Dead and the Gone*, is the companion to her young adult novel *Life As We Knew It*, a finalist for both the Andre Norton Award and the Quill Book Award. Ms. Pfeffer lives in Wallkill, New York, with her two Humane Society cats, Alexander and Emily.

## WHAT YOU CAN DO!

If you can't take a fuzzy friend home from your local animal shelter, become a weekend volunteer! Spend your Saturday walking dogs and playing with kittens. Then when you hear of friends or neighbors looking for a new pet, you can take them to the shelter and introduce them to your new friends!

# BE A VOICE FOR A RIVER

## By Nancy F. Castaldo

I grew up beside the Hudson River. Every day I saw the river out my window and as I walked to my school bus stop. I watched barges go by during the day and watched the sun set across the water at night. I lived in a watershed area where water drains off the land and flows into a river, even if that river is miles away. The rivers feed the lakes and the ocean and need to be kept clean.

Back in the 1960s, a Hudson River fisherman and congressional aide named John Cronin decided to patrol the river full-time. He became the voice of the river and the first river keeper in our country. There are now many river keepers and water keepers, and one of them probably patrols your local river.

They can't do the job alone, though. They need all of us to watch for changes in the water and for pollution being dumped into our streams and rivers.

We all have the right to clean water and we all have the responsibility to help protect that right. You can keep a lookout and volunteer for river keeper–sponsored cleanup days, but more importantly, get to know your river and streams. You might be the first one to notice when something is wrong, and then you can be a voice for your river. Find your local river keeper or water keeper at www.waterkeeper.org.

**NANCY CASTALDO** has picked up many rocks and climbed lots of trees. Now she spends most of her time writing books for kids. She is the author of several award-winning books and the recipient of the Art and Literature Award from the New York State Outdoor Education Association.

## WHAT YOU CAN DO!

Make sure there are "No Dumping" signs that are clear and easy to see near the rivers and streams in your town. And organize a community cleanup day once in a while to keep the area free of litter and the water free of pollutants.

# EGS

## By Roland Smith

Walk. I'm not kidding. You were designed to walk, and the earth was designed to be walked upon (not driven upon). This is one of the best things you can do to help the environment and yourself. Walking uses renewable clean energy—your energy—and it emits no pollution (unless you just ate a big bowl of chili before your walk).

When I was a kid (about two hundred years ago), I walked to school every day, kindergarten through eighth grade. We didn't have buses. My parents never drove me to school (not one time), nor did they pick me up after school. The school was about a mile away. As I walked, I picked up other "walkers" along the way. When we got to school, there was usually a gang of eight or nine of us. Sometimes it rained and we wore things called raincoats. Sometimes it snowed and we wore heavy coats, gloves, hats, and boots. We didn't have shoes with wheels like we do now, but our feet didn't care back then. We just put one foot in front of the other and arrived at our destination. Walking was how we got places.

People don't walk enough anymore. We drive to the mall or the grocery store, and cars wait for the closest parking place to the entrance, belching smoke and causing traffic snarls, when there are plenty of empty slots a hundred feet up the row.

When I go for a walk I rarely see anyone else walking. I bet five hundred people live within a five-mile radius of our rural neighborhood, probably more. I see (and feel) their cars zooming past. I see them peeking out the window at me as I walk by. But I never see them on their feet. When I walk to where I'm going, I arrive alone. I'm not sure what's happened, but we are afraid to use our legs. It's kind of sad. I think the earth misses the feel of our feet.

I try to walk a few miles every day no matter where I am. Sometimes I carry this tiny digital voice recorder with me and dictate my novels as I walk. (I actually dictated this piece about walking while I was walking.)

**ROLAND SMITH** is a former conservation biologist who has written twenty-five books, including *Peak, Elephant Run, Cryptid Hunters*, and *Zach's Lie*. There is a lot of walking in his adventure stories.

## WHAT YOU CAN DO!

Organize a community walk to raise money for a cause! Does your school need money for a recycling program? Ask your parents and friends and relatives to pledge one dollar for each half mile you walk.

# PART FOUR
# YOUR WORLD

## DID YOU KNOW?

• Even though the number of people living in the United States comprises only five percent of the world's population, U.S. residents use nearly a third of the world's resources and produce almost half of its hazardous waste.

• Every day fifty to one hundred species of animals and plants are driven to extinction by human influences.

• Rain forests are destroyed at a rate of about one hundred acres per minute. That's enough land to fill fifty football fields.

# Secret Karma

## By Matt de la Peña

When I was a kid growing up in San Diego, my family and I were helping to save the planet by default. No lie. We didn't have any money; therefore, we didn't waste a thing: not water, not heat, not gas, electricity, food, clothing, or paper. We were the epitome of the environmentally friendly family without even trying. The dangerous effects of global warming? The dwindling ozone layer? Man, we were just trying to pay the rent and keep food in the fridge. Then I went to college and graduate school and sold a few books—all of a sudden I have a couple of bucks in my pocket. But you know what's weird? I still live like I did when I was a kid. If I lived any other way I'd feel like a lazy, gluttonous sloth. I'm serious. I would disgust myself.

Each of us, you know, we only need so much.

I also have this weird superstition involving positive energy. Say I'm hustling for the subway because I'm late for a date. Say I toss a wad of paper toward the trash can and miss (which is extremely rare). I absolutely have to go scoop the paper wad out of the gutter and stick it in the trash. Call me an obsessive-compulsive person, but I literally can't function until my trash is in the can. Doesn't matter how late I am or how pretty the girl is who's waiting, I have to go back. Know why? Because I feel like if I litter—or run the shower too long or leave the AC humming while I'm out of the house or rent a gas-guzzling SUV—if I do any of these things, I'll mess up my positive energy flow with the planet and all my good luck will vanish. On the flip side, when I do my part for the environment I'm creating positive vibes with Mother Earth and she will continue looking out for me. Man, I know this sounds kind of hokey, and I've never ever explained it like this before (I feel sort of naked), but this is how my mind works. If I pick up my paper wad, finger roll it into the trash, luck will be on my side. Inspiration will hit the next time I sit down to work on my new writing project. My parents will maintain good health. I truly believe this.

That being said, I have a request: Let's go ahead and keep this information between you and me, okay? I don't need my Earth-saving-positive-energy theory getting out and people thinking I'm some kind of crazy weirdo. Maybe I'd never have another pretty girl waiting for me in the city. And I'll be honest, I really don't like the sound of that.

**MATT DE LA PEÑA** is the author of *Ball Don't Lie* and *Mexican WhiteBoy*. He lives in Brooklyn, New York.

# CAPTAIN MEAN-GREEN'S TEN RULES TO SAVE THE PLANET

## By Robert Lipsyte

Never flush the toilet.

When it gets hot in the house, walk around naked.

When it gets cold, take the blanket off your grandma's bed and wear it.

Always shut off other people's computers, iPods, and cell phone chargers if they are not paying attention.

Instead of stealing a car, sneak onto public transportation.

Don't ask for plastic or paper at the supermarket; slip food into your pockets before you get to the checkout.

Brush your teeth every other day: wash yourself every third day.

Use your sleeve instead of napkins.

Scratch "Save the Planet" on the hoods of SUVs.

Write shorter sentences to save trees.

Remember, kids—while Captain Mean-Green's rules are extreme, his message is clear: we all have to do our part to help save the environment and heal the damage that's been done to the planet.

**ROBERT LIPSYTE**, a former sports and city columnist for the *New York Times*, wrote the young adult novels *The Contender*, *Raiders Night*, and *Yellow Flag*.

# KID POWER

## By Susan Cooper

Kid power, that's what we need. Activists.

Once upon a time, I am ashamed to tell you, I smoked cigarettes, and the only person who was able to stop me was my daughter Kate. She was three years old at the time. She came home from nursery school one day and threw my brand-new pack of cigarettes into the garbage.

"What did you do that for?" I said, outraged.

"I don't want you to die," Kate said.

That was thirty-five years ago; today everyone knows about the nicotine-cancer link, and smoking is widely banned. Each generation of our flawed race has the job of correcting the mistakes made by the previous ones. Your job is the biggest yet; you have to stop global warming.

Start small, but *do* something, as Kate did. Check out your parents' environmental habits. Ask questions; create guilt. Do they throw out paper, plastic, cans, and glass without recycling them? Do they leave lights blazing in empty rooms? Drive gas-guzzling cars? Put chemical fertilizer on the lawn? Do they think green? Have they read Al Gore's book *An Inconvenient Truth* or rented the movie? Have you?

Check out your teachers, too. And your school. Ask them all the questions above, preferably in public. Start a club called Save the Planet, choose the ten best ideas in this book, and campaign for your whole town to adopt them. Write to newspapers and politicians. Take your club to the Internet; encourage other kids to start a Save the Planet group in their own school. Or if you prefer, join Kids for Saving Earth online. Make noise. Start small; go global.

Kid power, that's what we need.

**SUSAN COOPER** wrote the fantasy series The Dark Is Rising, among other things. She lives on an island in a salt marsh in Massachusetts.

## WHAT YOU CAN DO!

Think about changes you, your family, your school, and your community can make. Act on those changes, or find an adult who can help you. Make a difference in your world.

# Earth Rules! (And Some Simple Rules for Life on Earth!)

## By Rafe Martin

If you enjoy your life, you'll want to take care of our home, the earth, by making decisions that allow for meaningful living. So thank the air and thank the water every day! Thank our food, and be grateful for the healthy life it gives us.

Periodically hold a potluck dinner and read aloud with friends, just for the joy of it. The less TV the better—for so many reasons, including to have more fun. Isn't that the whole point?

This is an easy rule to follow. It's like saying having fun is a good way to help the earth. Find a community of friends to share your life with, and don't forget to get out and actually do things with them. The less lonely we are, the less we'll end up depending on things we have to buy to make us happy, the less destruction of the environment there'll be.

I try to avoid buying unnecessary things. The more that is manufactured that isn't actually needed, the more waste and pollution are created. Balancing needs and wants, desires and plain old wishes for more "stuff," can be fun. I try to make a game of it, asking myself, "Do I really need this? Can it wait? Or is there a good reason to get it now?"

Final rules: Read and write. Tell stories. (They build community!) Walk up mountains. Kayak on rivers. Stand on ladders and put in low-energy fluorescent bulbs. Sing and dance.

Let's be environmentally aware, and at the same time, let's have a good time being alive here on our beautiful planet! If we do, I think we'll be much more sure to take good care of our world. And if we take care of the earth, it will continue to take care of us, giving us all we need to live a meaningful life.

**RAFE MARTIN** is the award-winning author of more than twenty books, including *The Rough-Face Girl*, *Will's Mammoth*, *The World Before This One*, and *Birdwing*.

# A HOUSE WITH A ROUND DOOR

## By Jeanne DuPrau

Not far from where I live, there used to be a magnificent euca-lyptus tree, taller than a five-story building. Its branches made an entire world for birds. Sometimes in the evening, when I walked past that tree, I saw a family of great horned owls. They sat on a high branch and gazed sternly down at me with their round yellow eyes. In the spring I saw their babies, little fluff balls sitting on the branches next to their parents. Often in the night I would hear the owls calling to each other: *whoo-hoo, hoo, hoo*. I loved those owls. They were so beautiful and strange.

Some years later, houses were built all around the area where that tree grew. Beneath the tree, instead of a field of grass, there was a big house with a lawn. The tree remained for a while, towering over the house. Then one day when I walked by, only a flat stump stood where the tree had been. Probably the people in the house worried that the tree's huge branches might break in a storm and fall on their roof. (I wondered: Why didn't they think of this before they bought the house?) The owls disappeared.

If I could provide a tree for the owls in my backyard, I'd do it. But it takes many years for a tree to grow, and acres of fields to hold enough mice and gophers for owls to hunt. So instead, I'm trying to make sure that other birds don't run out of places to live. I've hung a birdhouse on a wall outside my living room. It has a little green roof and a round hole of the correct size—big enough for a small bird to fly through but too small for a larger bird (or a rat) that might be looking for an egg dinner.

For two years, chickadees have raised a family in my birdhouse. As the mom and dad chickadees go about their nest-building and egg-sitting business, I watch them from my window. Last summer, I happened to be watching at the very moment the babies decided it was time to leave the nest. One after the other, they poked their heads from the little round door and made the leap, fluttering into the branches of the nearby apricot tree. Yay! Four brand-new chickadees added to the world!

My birdhouse won't bring back the owls. It's just a small thing, giving a home to a chickadee family. But all over the world, places for birds to live are disappearing, while places for people to live spread and spread. To be healthy and whole, our world needs all its creatures, not just human beings. It feels good to try to balance things out a little.

**JEANNE DUPRAU** is the author of *The City of Ember* and other books. She lives in California, where she has not only a birdhouse but a birdbath and a garden full of flowers that hummingbirds love.

## WHAT YOU CAN DO!

For every tree that has to come down in your community, advocate for the planting of another. Have a parent or teacher help you speak to the town council to find a good place for one.

# BEACH BLUES

## By Marcie Aboff

I love the beach. Ever since I was young, I've had so many great memories of jumping in the waves, building sand castles, and collecting seashells. Now that I have my own kids, we all love "going down the shore," as we say here in New Jersey. But with global warming increasing, miles of beaches are becoming eroded as the sea level gets higher and higher. Many reports estimate that as the polar ice caps melt, the sea level will keep rising and rising and thousands of miles of beaches could eventually be washed away!

I hate the idea of losing our beaches! Since the biggest cause of global warming is the carbon dioxide released when fossil fuels like oil and coal are burned for energy, we need to drive less—carpool more. When my kids have soccer games or dance rehearsals or other places they need to go, we carpool with others in the group (your parents will like this one, too—they won't have to drive as much). Or if it's close by, you can ride your bike or skateboard . . . or walk!

You could also remind your parents to buy energy-efficient appliances and use the newer compact fluorescent lightbulbs. These new lightbulbs last ten times as long as standard lightbulbs and keep tons of carbon dioxide out of the air! (They save money, too.) And if you think one person can't make a difference, think again.

There's a great story that has become a folktale of sorts about a little girl and a starfish on the beach. One day, a man is walking along the beach where thousands of starfish have been left stranded by the tide. As he walks, he comes across a little girl who is picking up the dying starfish. One by one, she is throwing them back into the ocean. The man says, "Look at how many starfish there are. You can't possibly throw them all back into the ocean before they die. You're wasting your time. It's not going to make a difference."

And the little girl replies as she throws another starfish back into the ocean, "It made a difference to that one."

Now it's *your* turn to make a difference!

**MARCIE ABOFF** is the author of more than forty books for young readers. She gets her inspiration for writing by talking with kids, reading, and imagining, "What if?"—and by spending time at the beach.

# Buying New Stuff

## By Jerry Spinelli

I was at a mall the other day, with hundreds of other people, all of us shopping. And I saw on the cover of a book the face of a poor mother who lives in a so-called Third World country. And suddenly I was seeing this whole mall scene through her eyes, and she was saying things like "What are these people doing?" and "Where are they?" and "Shopping? What is shopping?"

It is all the poor mother can do to obtain food and a few rags of clothing for herself and her baby. She cannot imagine "going shopping." I looked around. Flocks of people were laughing, eating, browsing the shops, holding out their hands to ATMs. Shopping in middle-class America is fun. Recreation. Entertainment. Buying new stuff.

Buying new stuff.

How often do we ask ourselves: Do I really need this? ("Of course I need it. Liz and Jen each have one. How can I not need it?") How often do we use something until it breaks or wears out before replacing it? Or ask ourselves if it really needs to be replaced at all?

Buying new stuff.

Not only do we more often buy according to our wants rather than our needs, amazingly, we often buy stuff that we don't even especially want! We just love to buy.

Buying new stuff. It's a national attitude. A national bad habit. A national addiction. A couple of cures:

1. Find other ways to have fun.
2. Buy stuff at thrift shops.
3. Donate your own used stuff to Goodwill and places like that.
4. Remember the poor mother.

**JERRY SPINELLI** is the author of many books, including the Newbery Medal–winning *Maniac Magee*, the Newbery Honor Book *Wringer*, and the *New York Times* bestselling books *Stargirl* and *Love, Stargirl*.

# HARKY

## By Graham Salisbury

When I was twelve, we moved from Oahu to the Big Island of Hawaii, where I discovered a whole new world . . . under water. One day, I grabbed my speargun and swam out looking for deep water. I saw eels, parrot fish, a small manta half buried in the sand, and hundreds of multicolored fish grazing around mossy colonies of coral. It was stunning.

I speared five or six good fish for eating and strung them on a length of fishing line tied to my waist. I was hot stuff, for sure.

Until I saw the shark.

It wasn't a big one, maybe five or six feet. Gray. Lazy. Poking its nose in and out of crevasses. Looking for fish to eat . . . like the ones dangling from my dragline, leaking blood.

I froze, thinking: *I'm dead.*

The shark nosed closer, eyeing me. My hands started to tremble. I dropped the speargun and clumsily ripped my dragline free. *Here, sharky, sharky, eat these nice fat fish, and not me.*

Slowly, I stroked closer to shore, leaving the fish behind. The shark watched, curious. He probably had no intention of snacking on me, but I swore he was licking his lips.

That day I got lucky. The shark let me swim to shore untouched. But really, what if I'd met up with little sharky's daddy? And what if he'd been more than just curious? For sure, the Universe was watching over me.

What does this have to do with solving the problems of our planet? Simply this: everything.

Sharky taught me something. He taught me to be aware. It's amazing how many people aren't. And I was one of them.

The absolute most important thing I've done to help protect the planet is to develop an awareness of the need to do my part. Now I see all kinds of things I can do to conserve, preserve, use more wisely, nurture, and protect.

Sharky is out there.

Be aware, and care. The brightest hope for our planet is you. And me.

**GRAHAM SALISBURY** is the author of *Under the Blood-Red Sun*, *Eyes of the Emperor*, *Night of the Howling Dogs*, and other books for young readers. He lives in Portland, Oregon, with his family.

# WHEN IN DOUBT, DON'T

## By Daniel Pinkwater

Given a small country with few inhabitants . . . though there should be among the people contrivances requiring ten times, a hundred times less labor, they would not use them. . . . There might still be boats and carriages, but no one would go in them; there might still be weapons of war, but no one would drill with them. . . . The people should have no use for any form of writing save knotted ropes, should be contented with their food, pleased with their clothing, satisfied with their homes, should take pleasure in their rustic tasks. The next place might be so near at hand that one could hear the cocks crowing in it, the dogs barking; but the

people would grow old and die without ever having
been there.

—Lao-tzu, *Tao-te Ching*,
translated by Arthur Waley

Even in the sixth century B.C., when Lao-tzu wrote those words, the quiet village life he describes was probably already impossible—but he presents it as a goal worth keeping in sight. *Tao-te Ching* is my favorite book, and the favorite of a lot of other people. It has been translated more times than any other book except the Bible. It is a book of . . . I don't know . . . philosophy, advice to a ruler, a way to live . . . different people have different ideas about it. One of the ideas in the book is the idea of not-doing. You can usually avoid problems if you don't stir things up.

When in doubt, don't! Rushing around can get you in trouble. Having a big gas-guzzling pollution-emitting car is not a bad thing if you never start it up. Being in the habit of overconsuming is how we hurt the earth—finding out that we can enjoy it without trying to consume it is how we can help it.

**DANIEL PINKWATER** is the author of many books, such as *Fat Men from Space*, *The Hoboken Chicken Emergency*, and *Once Upon a Blue Moose*. He is also a regular commentator on National Public Radio.

# NOOSES, MUZZLES, AND JELLYFISH

## By Sara Pennypacker

I live on Cape Cod, which sticks out from the state of Massachusetts like a curled arm making a fist. (I like to think of this fist as holding something really nice—M&M's, maybe, or something safe—not as getting ready to punch something.) Whenever I walk on one of the beautiful beaches here, I bring along a bag to collect plastic litter. I don't do this to keep the beaches looking clean and pretty—although that's a nice side benefit—but because plastic litter in the ocean is so dangerous to marine and shore animals.

It's estimated that one hundred thousand marine mammals and turtles are killed by plastic litter every year; even more birds and fish. Many are starved by being muzzled—those plastic rings that hold soda cans together are especially dangerous, even to animals as large as seals and dolphins. Lots more animals get trapped or strangled by larger pieces, like netting or plastic ropes. And many creatures mistake plastic bags or balloons for jellyfish or squid or other things they like to eat and swallow them by mistake; then the bags and balloons are deadly because they can choke the animals or block their digestive systems. Recently a whale was found dead because a large plastic bottle had blocked its intestines. Think of that: One plastic bottle that weighed less than an ounce, tossed into the ocean in a second of carelessness, killed an enormous, beautiful whale. And worse still: It's not just one animal a piece of plastic can kill! Because an animal will decompose much faster than plastic will, a piece of plastic litter that kills an animal will be floating around again soon afterward, so it can kill other animals.

Do you live near a body of water, or visit one? Wherever there is water—rivers and streams, ponds and lakes, oceans and seas—there are animals who depend on us to keep their environments safe. Picking up plastic trash is an easy way to help.

**SARAH PENNYPACKER** has written many books for kids. She likes to write those books while she's walking on the beach.

## WHAT YOU CAN DO!

Clean up litter wherever you see it! Talk to a parent or teacher to try to institute a town or school cleanup day a couple of times a year.

# TURNING WORRY INTO ACTION

## By Karen Cushman

What do I do? I worry, and I get angry. Sure, I do ordinary helpful things, like taking short showers, carrying my green cloth bags for groceries, and keeping the heat turned so low that icicles form on my husband's nose. But it does not feel like enough, and I worry. I worry about tsunamis and droughts, melting polar ice caps and toxic waste, polar bears and sea turtles, and the children. Oh, how I worry about the children who must live in the world that we leave them.

So I grow angry. I throw my slippers at those newsmen on television who underestimate the issue and those politicians who dismiss, delay, or deny. Then I take a deep breath and use my anger to try to make change. I carry signs, write letters, and sign petitions. Most important of all, I vote. I vote for candidates who make this Earth and its people a priority, who not only talk about pollution and global warming but do something about it, who risk their political lives to protect this planet and all of us who live here.

And I encourage you to ask your parents to do the same, to vote for candidates who make Earth a priority. Do it for the polar bears and the sea turtles and for yourselves, for this world belongs to you.

**KAREN CUSHMAN** is the author of the Newbery Award–winning book *The Midwife's Apprentice* and other books of historical fiction. When she is not writing or worrying or voting, she sits by the window and watches the rain.

# WHEN THE RAIN REFUSES TO FALL

## By Mem Fox

Here in Australia we almost have no water left, so we're dead keen to use it as wisely as possible. Most of us have a bucket in the shower to catch the water while it heats up, which we use afterward on the garden. Most of us have a crazy plastic kind of pipe thing attached to our washing machines so the gray water (any water that has been used in the home, except toilet water) goes straight on to the trees in the garden. This means we have to use Earth-friendly detergents in our washing machines.

No new house in our state can be built without a rainwater tank that is plumbed into the home. And most of us, even those in posh houses, dry our clothes outside on a very tasteful clothesline to save the environment and to have the sweet smell of sun on our sheets and pillowcases.

Kids can certainly do this: Have a four-minute timer in the shower itself or in the bathroom, and, to save even more time and water, take the tops off the shampoo bottles before you turn on the water.

I drive a tiny car so as not to pollute the world more than I have to, and to preserve the oil that the world is quickly running out of. An increasing number of us have solar panels on our roofs. Our parliament building (the equivalent of your state legislature building) has wind power on its roof.

I think kids should also ensure that their sandwiches, wraps, etc., are wrapped in wax paper, not plastic wrap. And they should aim, when they grow up, to live in smaller houses that are close to shopping centers so they can ride bikes or walk to the store. If possible, they should ask for trees to be planted in their gardens, since trees are wonderful for cooling and warming houses naturally without air-conditioning, which uses too many of the world's precious resources.

**MEM FOX** is Australia's most renowned writer for young children. She is a very keen pacifist as well as an environment freak.

# KEEP PLASTIC TO YOURSELF

## By Stephen R. Swinburne

I'm saving every piece of plastic I use. Every coffee lid, straw, foam cup, plastic bag, plastic utensil, bottle cap, old CD. My family thinks I'm crazy, but I'm a guy who regularly checks roadkill for positive ID, so go figure. We recycle everything at our Vermont house, but tons of plastic in our lives still gets thrown away, so I'm keeping my plastic to myself. I now have three fifty-five-gallon garbage bags of plastic in my barn. When I go on a trip, I bring home crumpled water bottles and plastic take-out containers in my luggage. I won't throw this stuff away until someone comes up with a way to use it. Plastic comes from oil and lasts forever. Every piece of plastic manufactured for the last fifty years or so, unless it's been incinerated or recycled, is still on the planet somewhere. A lot of this plastic ends up in the ocean, eventually breaking down into tiny bits of plastic called *nurdles*. In some parts of the ocean, there's more plastic than plankton. Sea turtles are suffocated when they chomp on plastic bags thinking they're jellyfish, their favorite food. And ocean birds wash up dead on beaches with bellies full of plastic bottle caps. So will one of you kids *please* come up with a way to use my leftover plastic? Or better yet, figure out how to make plastic out of something other than oil, something that will biodegrade, like recycled road-kill or old sneakers or something. I'm running out of room in the barn.

When not hoarding plastic, **STEPHEN R. SWINBURNE** visits schools around the country and writes nonfiction books, including *Saving Manatees*, *Once a Wolf*, and *Turtle Tide*.

# SLAYING DRAGONS WITH VOTES

## By Elvira Woodruff

When I was growing up, we lived in an apartment across the street from a very big factory in New Jersey. My dad drove a truck in and out of the factory every day. Most of my friends' fathers worked there as well. At night the factory would light up like some giant monster with all kinds of colored lights. My sisters and I would call it the Dragon. It was quite a show going on right outside our bedroom window. I'd make up all kinds of stories for my sisters about the Dragon and how powerful it was.

During the day this dragon was so powerful that it could turn our summers into winter. Often on a dry, warm day you could see bits of white fluff in the air coming from the factory's smokestacks. All the kids in the neighborhood would pretend

217

it was snow and we'd run outside and try to catch it. My mother and the other moms in town had no idea that the snow could hurt us. They didn't know that the factory was a monster after all, for the product it made was called asbestos, which can make you very sick and eventually kill you. Though the owners of the factory knew that asbestos was harmful to people, animals, and the earth, they kept this information a secret. They cared more about making money than protecting people and the earth.

Years later my father and many of my friends and their families suffered with a disease that attacks the lungs called asbestosis. I am still angry at the men who cared more about making money than about making their workplace safe. Today when I vote for a candidate, I check his or her record on environmental issues first. I want to make sure that candidate will do everything in his or her power to keep the monsters from ruining any more lives. Ask your parents whom they are voting for and what their candidate's record on the environment is. Today I use my votes to slay dragons whenever I can. When it's time for you to vote, I hope you'll do the same.

**ELVIRA WOODRUFF** is the author of more than twenty books, including *George Washington's Socks*, *The Ravenmaster's Secret: Escape from the Tower of London*, and *The Magnificent Mummy Maker*. Her most recent book is *Fearless*.

## WHAT YOU CAN DO!

Talk to your parents about whom they'll be voting for in community, state, and national elections. It's never too soon to think about the types of leaders you want to influence your future.

# Our Small Corner of the Planet

## By Laurie Halse Anderson

My family works to stay mindful of our use of limited resources. The best moment of the past year was when we sold
my husband's truck. He is now a carpenter who drives a
Subaru (good mileage!) to haul his tools around. I drive a
Honda Fit, which we bought for its incredible gas mileage and
low emissions. And we rarely use our cars for a single trip.
Instead we plan out the week and combine trips to the store,
bank, library, and everyplace else.

We belong to a community-supported agriculture co-op
and try to buy only food that is produced within a fifty-mile
radius of our home. I spent most of last August canning and
freezing fruits and vegetables so we wouldn't have to buy

produce grown in California or South America (and transported thousands of miles) when the snow started.

Our land is not the best for growing things, but we have been building up the soil with compost and hope to be gardening on it soon. We are also talking about raising chickens and maybe other critters. We are not vegetarians; we love eating meat. But we try to support regional farmers who raise their animals humanely (i.e., grass-fed, free-range). My husband also hunts deer and turkey.

Some people think we're crazy, but we keep our house at sixty degrees in the winter. (It really isn't that hard to get used to.) We heat it mostly with a special enclosed fireplace designed to burn clean and radiate lots of warmth. The emissions from the fireplace are offset by the positive contribution the trees make to the environment when they are growing. We do not have an air conditioner. Instead we use the basement more during the summer; it's nice and cool there when it gets hot outside.

We make a game out of how little electricity we can get by with. We've changed all our bulbs to compact fluorescents and use energy-efficient appliances. We do not use hair dryers. We rarely use the clothes dryer. We line-dry, even hanging up wet clothes inside during the winter. Right now we're saving our money to purchase a windmill so we can generate our own electricity.

We try to live our life so that it truly reflects our values;

our spirituality in action. We want the seventh generation of the seventh generation of our children to live in health and abundance in a world that has been restored to balance.

**LAURIE HALSE ANDERSON** is the *New York Times* bestselling author of *Speak*, which earned a National Book Award nomination, a Michael L. Printz Honor, and numerous ALA and state awards. Laurie lives in northern New York, where she likes to watch the snow fall as she writes.

# RECYCLING OUR THINKING

## By Ferida Wolff

I wasn't brought up to think about the environment. I grew up in the city and didn't know anything about farming. I never questioned where the food I was eating came from. Most of the vegetables I ate came from cans. I assumed that was the way everyone ate.

But when I had my own children, I knew it was important to give them the best food, the healthiest food I could. I found out that organically grown food was what I wanted. I chose organic food because organic farmers don't use pesticides or other chemicals that can end up in the plants and then in our bodies.

Some of my family said, "Why bother?" And it was a bother. I had trouble finding stores that carried anything organic. So I joined a group of people who also wanted organic food for their families. Every two weeks a truck from an organic farm delivered organic fruits and vegetables to a member's garage and we all went to pick up our food. I had to buy enough produce to last until the truck came back again.

But I discovered that organic farming is a lot more important than I realized. It helps to keep the soil in which our food is grown healthy, too. Healthy soil is like a community. It has nutrients and worms and insects all working together in a balanced ecosystem. Recycling organic material like manure and compost helps keep the soil nutrient-rich and usable for a long time. When artificial chemicals are added to produce a bigger crop, the living parts of the community diminish and the soil gets used up, which throws the community out of balance. It isn't good for people or the earth.

I talked to my friends about organic foods. I told them the reasons I support organic farms and eat organic. Lots of people besides me also were talking about organic food. Some specialty markets started offering it. Now most regular supermarkets carry at least some organic products because their customers began asking for it and they see that people will buy it.

Even though I didn't grow up knowing anything about organic food, I shifted my thinking as an adult about what I eat and how I live and I acted on those new thoughts. Anyone can think in new ways, at any age. Thoughts are powerful. When people change their thinking, society changes. We don't have to stay stuck in old thoughts. Recycling our thinking can lead to new actions that sustain rather than harm ourselves and our beautiful Earth.

**FERIDA WOLFF** is the author of seventeen books for young readers and two books of essays for adults. Her essays appear in newspapers and magazines, and she is a frequent contributor to the Chicken Soup for the Soul series.

# A VIEW FROM THE TOP OF THE WORLD

## By Shelley Gill

I live in Alaska and see the effects of global warming all around me. It is December as I write this. My view eight years ago from my log cabin was a snowbound fantasy. A typical Christmas included sledding on the hard-packed eight feet of white stuff. Today it is forty-one degrees and the brown stalks of fireweed are matted into a moldy sodden carpet. No snow. The brown bears are still out because it's too warm to den up.

In the summer I work as a humpback whale researcher in Prince William Sound. The water temperature there has increased each summer, so that now we are beginning to see new species such as dolphins and bull sharks, which are not typically found in these waters. The Arctic pack ice is

226

melting; the algae bloom is sinking each spring instead of feeding the plankton and krill that sustain the whales, so they are beginning to stay longer and longer, feeding on ever more meager schools of herring and krill.

So what can we do?

On a personal level I have given up treats like tomatoes from Chile and strawberries from Mexico. I eat the food I grow or catch in the summer. I bought half a cow from a neighbor and traded boarding a friend's horse for moose and halibut. I'm lucky because I am pretty self-sufficient. You can't live this way in the city . . . or can you? I think about all the vacant littered lots I have seen in every city I ever visited. Why don't those cities offer tax incentives to the owners to host community vegetable gardens, plant fruit- and nut-bearing trees, or establish parks?

If you live where the wind blows, put in a windmill. If you live where a stream flows, build your own simple waterwheel hydro plant. We need to fight back and our government needs to help us. If we applied a fraction of the money we spent on the Iraq War to developing clean energy, we would be well on our way. We need to elect politicians who are environmentally minded. To do that we need to speak up and spell it out. No more waste. As consumers we have the obligation to demand less packaging, higher quality, and more recycled products. Refuse to buy junk.

When my daughter Kye was nine, she told me, "Mom, I

have enough stuff. From now on, I want an adventure!" From that point on we dug up dinosaurs, swam with a blue whale, and climbed every peak we could find.

Our entire culture has literally been sold a bill of goods. We are in debt, overfed, and nearly dead from overconsuming. It is time to put on the brakes, be thoughtful, and ask not how the planet can sustain us, but how we can begin to sustain her.

SHELLEY GILL has written twenty-three children's books, including *Tongass—The Last American Rainforest*, *Big Blue*, *Swimmer*, and *Thunderfeet*. She is an Iditarod musher, whale detective, and eco-warrior and recently spent months studying the rapidly melting ice and at-risk fauna of Antarctica. She lives in Homer, Alaska.

## WHAT YOU CAN DO!

Start small, but think big! Plant a garden in your backyard. Organize a Green Day in your community where neighbors can clean up, clear out, and overall make their home a cleaner, more eco-safe environment to live in.

# **S**HOUT

## By Bruce Balan

I started recycling cans and bottles and aluminum foil twenty-five years ago when I had to haul them down to the recycling center myself—they weren't picked up at the curb with the trash.

I bought compact fluorescent lightbulbs when they were first available.

I kept the thermostat turned down in my house.

When I had a car, I drove one that got good mileage.

And you know what? The environment is worse off now than it was before I did all those things. I'm only one person, and it seems like what I do doesn't make a dent.

So what does?

Speaking up.

Shouting out.

Letting your voice be heard.

That's what.

I bother family and friends.

I turn off the lights they leave on. And make them notice.

I close the refrigerator door when they don't. And I tell them about it.

I move the soda can—noisily—from the trash where they dropped it to the recycling bin where it belongs.

I suggest they put solar panels on their roof instead of buying a new television.

I let them know they should be ashamed for driving an SUV.

And I don't just bother the people I know.

I leave bumper stickers under windshield wipers on SUVs I see in parking lots. The stickers say: "Your children are dying so I can drive this car."

That's true, you know. Adults are destroying your world. So let them know about it. Shout it out. Get in their face. It's your world and it's up to you to tell us how to treat it.

Save the world by speaking up.

Yep, reduce, reuse, and recycle—we all need to do our part.

But our part is also helping everyone else to do their part.

Don't be shy.

Speak up.
Save your world.

**BRUCE BALAN** writes as he sails around the world in his sailboat, which is powered by the wind and uses solar panels to generate electricity. He no longer owns a car or a house. He always votes. Bruce is the author of fourteen books.

# A JUNGLE VILLAGE: THEN, NOW, AND FUTURE

## By William Sleator

I live with my Thai family in a remote village in Thailand. We grow our own rice, using no pesticides. We grow our own vegetables and chili peppers (which are an absolute essential in Thai food). We have our own banana and mango trees. In mango season there are too many mangoes for us to eat, so my sister-in-law makes a paste out of the mangoes, spreads it on trays, and dries it in the sun. It is the most delicious mango candy I've ever eaten. We have our own chickens that run around the yard, and of course our own eggs. We have a large tank where we farm fish—tiny fish get big enough to eat in three months. The rest of the family relishes eating rats and large fried insects (I don't), but eating them is better than having them running around the house.

When we bought the land it had been a rice field, but now it is full of trees we planted—our own jungle. The house is surrounded by bougainvilleas that bloom all year round. We have our own well, which is 120 feet deep. They had to bore through stone to get that far down, but man, the water is clean! We are almost completely self-sufficient. We do have a car, but mostly we use a motorcycle because it doesn't use anywhere near as much gas as a car.

We live this way because it's cheaper, and because everything we grow ourselves is better than what you can buy. But we also just enjoy living like this, and we feel so safe here! If civilization collapsed, we could still go on living here in mostly the same way. And it's good to know that we are breathing air that has no pollution.

When I first came to Thailand, years ago, I lived for two years in Bangkok, the capital city. It is one of the most congested and polluted cities in the world. The traffic is so bad that it takes forever to get anywhere. If you're riding in a taxi, you can get out of the taxi, walk into a store, wait in line to buy a pack of gum, go back outside, and the taxi will still be in the same place, stuck in traffic. Now that we have our house in the village, I can't stand the city anymore.

The village is still changing. There are more houses all the time. Someday there will be factories. Someday there will be traffic and pollution. But because we have our own land

and our own farm, we can keep living in the same way forever, no matter what happens around us. And we know we're not doing anything to damage the climate, or the planet.

**WILLIAM SLEATOR** is the author of many science-fiction novels, including *House of Stairs*, *The Boy Who Couldn't Die*, and *Interstellar Pig*.

# A BEACH IS MADE OF MANY SMALL PIECES OF SAND

## By Mike Shoulders

What do I do to help the environment? A better question might be: What *don't* I do? And I don't believe I'm alone in this battle.

The U.S. Army recently used the slogan "An Army of One." It makes sense to me because every one of us makes a difference. It's important for us not to lose sight of the fact that we are all foot soldiers, part of a global army waging war to protect our planet. I don't think I'm going to do one big thing that will solve this problem. But I do believe that we, by doing many small things, are solving problems together.

For instance, when I purchase one or two items at the

store, I never take the bag. Clerks sometimes are taken aback. But I remind myself that there are probably a thousand customers around the world doing the exact same thing at the exact same time: refusing to take an unneeded bag that will end up in the landfill.

What do I do to help the environment? I don't forget I'm part of a global army. That gives me hope. That gives me strength. That reassures me that we are making a difference, one person, one act at a time.

No gesture is too small or is unappreciated! After all, a beach is made of many small grains of sand.

**MIKE SHOULDERS** is the author of *Say Daddy!* He loves the beach and always leaves it cleaner than when he arrived.

## WHAT YOU CAN DO!

Remember that you are part of a global community. What you put into the world and what you take out of it will affect people you may never think about or even meet.

# You, me, us

## By Kathleen Duey

I think the most important thing anyone can do to save our beautiful planet is to believe that we can. It really is up to us. And every little bit helps.

Where I live, water is scarce, and it's becoming scarce in a lot of places. It's very easy to use less. You can save fifteen to twenty gallons every week if you turn off the faucet while you brush your teeth, wash your face, gel your hair, do the zit check in the mirror, put dishes in the dishwasher, and soap up in the shower. You can run only full loads in the dishwasher, and wash only clothes that really need it. It's simple, and you will be saving 1,040 gallons of water a year. And if just half of all Americans join you, more than 156 billion gallons of water a year will still be in the reservoirs, the wells, the lakes, the rivers.

You will reduce other kinds of pollution at the same time—less pumping and less heating = less carbon dioxide pollution to influence Earth's climate.

Once you start to think about it, the ideas are almost endless. Drive less, walk more. When you leave your room, turn off your computer, flip off the light. Don't buy products that poison our air and water. Don't waste food. Buy cloth shopping bags and take them to the store. Every single thing you do helps save your family, your friends, your planet—and yourself. Believe it and it can happen.

**KATHLEEN DUEY** lives in California and writes for middle-grade and young adult readers. She is currently working on a novel about a young man who lives in a world people are desperately trying to escape.

## WHAT YOU CAN DO!

Believe that change is possible. Speak up, take action, make small changes in your home or school. It starts with you.

# THE TEMPERATURE IS RISING

## By Jack Prelutsky

The temperature is rising,
No matter where you roam.
The Earth is getting warmer,
Our one and only home.
The world may soon experience
A cataclysmic change
As everything upon its face
Begins to rearrange.

And as the poles grow warmer,
And all the glaciers melt,
There will not be a single spot
Where this will not be felt.

Our planet could become a place
We simply do not know,
And polar bears and penguins
Will have nowhere left to go.

**JACK PRELUTSKY** lives in the Pacific Northwest. He has written more than forty books of verse and compiled eleven poetry anthologies. In 2006 the Poetry Foundation named him the nation's first Children's Poet Laureate.

# NOUGH

## By Floyd Cooper

I turn off lights.

I carefully separate the family garbage: plastic and glass in yellow bins, newspapers neatly stacked and tied.

Yet it doesn't seem quite enough.

I shower at Guinness World Record speed.

I use squiggly lightbulbs, recycle, recover, reuse, unplug, compost, drive electric hybrids, choose paper over plastic, carpool, take the bus, ditch the Styrofoam, picket the polluters!

And I still can't help feeling it's not enough.

Nightmares of Native American tears, while snuggled in woolly-blanket bedtimes in winter, don't lessen my fears.

Sticky summers with oscillating fans while ice caps continue to melt only add to my worries.

It seems useless to use less.

Until I realize that you, my friend, are reading this. And if you care as much as I do, and do some of these things, too, then maybe it isn't so impossible after all.

Maybe the trees that fall in the rain forest will make the sounds that summon us to save things for us.

To save this Earth for us. *To save us.*

**FLOYD COOPER** was born in Tulsa and spent many summers in and around farms and country homes in Bixby, Muskogee, and Haskell, Oklahoma, where he discovered a way of life in which he becomes less of a consumer and more of a saver of Earth's fragile resources.

# USE LESS STUFF!

## By Tony Abbott

I have a confession to make.

Back on New Year's Eve in 1999, I had a secret wish that computers unable to read the date 2000 would explode from one time zone to the next all the way around the globe until we were plunged into a preindustrial world of horses, hand rakes, wide-scale poverty, and rotting fruit.

Not really. I didn't wish for such a disaster. The results would have been unthinkable. But imagining what could have happened helped me imagine something else. If we were suddenly without the stuff we're used to, we'd think twice before misusing what we do have. We might end up using less of everything. And planet Earth might be better for it.

Think of everything you use as if we were running out of

it. Try not running the faucet needlessly. If you stop the water while brushing your teeth, you'll end up not only conserving water, but also brushing longer. If you imagine you are using what might be the last of something, you'll be surprised how much more thoughtfully you act.

Squeeze out the absolute last dab of toothpaste before tossing the tube. Cut open the end of the tube if you have to! Take a second to inspect every scrap of paper before tossing it in the trash, to see if you can still use it. Believe me, I have written some of my best ideas on old envelopes, the flip sides of grocery lists, the backs of business cards, even my own hand (but only I can use that!). Sharpen your pencil until there's nothing left. Use the kind of pen that takes refills. It may be uncool, but we're in critical mode here.

If your town doesn't recycle plastic and glass and paper, save up your own and take it to the nearest recycling center once every two months.

And what about water? My gosh, water! Now, I'm not about to save bathwater to make soup, but I'm pretty sure we can all take shorter showers. Try cutting your time by a third, then a half. Try to get it down to five minutes. Lather, rinse, get out. That's still a lot of water falling on you. And, after all, how big are you?

Consider the luxury we live in, and consider that someday it may end, if not for us, then for those after us. How should we do things differently? Use less stuff, that's how. So write it down: "Use Less Stuff." Paste it on your desk. Tape it to your bathroom mirror. Stick it to your refrigerator. Stopping waste shouldn't be a task; it should be an attitude we all share. There's something happily natural about it. And it's good for our world.

**TONY ABBOTT** is the author of the fantasy series the Secrets of Droon and the novel *Firegirl*, winner of the Golden Kite Award for Fiction. He lives in Connecticut.

# CHOOSE WELL

## By Donna Jo Napoli

People can make you lists of things to do, and you can try to memorize those lists and go for it. But the opportunities to plunder the earth keep multiplying; new ones pop up daily. So, really, the point is for you to look at the world honestly and figure out how you can live decently on this planet.

If you need something, well, you need it. And there are many different kinds of needs. But there are plenty of things you might sort of want that you don't need—and it takes energy to make all those things. If we are more selective about what we reach for, fewer things will be made and fewer resources will be sapped, freeing up those resources for meeting necessities.

And even if you have strong needs, there are choices

about how to satisfy your needs. Disposable things are often a terrible choice (Bottled water? Give me a break). Things that use limited resources are often a terrible choice (Clothes dryers? The sun is there—hang out your laundry).

You may think it doesn't matter whether human beings remain on Earth. That is certainly debatable. But what's not debatable is that if we continue our mindless and wasteful greed, the amount of suffering we are already causing to life on Earth is going to increase savagely. The extinction of humanity (and polar bears and gorillas and you-name-it) will not be a quiet light switch turning off. It will be the loudest, longest cry of agony there ever was.

Go green because it is the only thing worth doing.

**DONNA JO NAPOLI** is a mother, dancer, gardener, baker, linguist, and grandmother. She has written many books for children of all ages.

# BIT BY BIT BY BIT

## By DyAnne DiSalvo

Every little bit helps, that's what I think. And so whenever I think I am not doing enough to help the earth, I remind myself of the little things I do. I don't spit my gum on the sidewalk. I always shove candy paper in my pockets. And I don't leave the water running when I brush my teeth. I also recycle my revised manuscripts into a toy for my dog, Buddy. Buddy tears up my manuscript pages into bits and pieces. When he is through having fun, I bag up the paper for the recycling bin. You can try this with your homework when you get frustrated; it is a satisfying mess if you don't mind cleaning it up. It's like recycling twice.

Another little thing I do is recycle my guitar strings. I

give them to a local art studio for bead strings to make into jewelry. It might not seem like much, but I change my guitar strings three times a month; that adds up to 216 strings a year. Plus my husband is a musician, and he does the same thing with his electric guitar strings. So you can see where this is going.

Have you ever thought about cleaning up an empty lot and turning it into a garden? I have. As you might have noticed, there are a lot of new houses being built these days. Not that I am against houses. Everyone needs a place to live. But what about those empty spaces where there used to be a house and now there is nothing but junk? Cleaning up a vacant lot is another little way of making your neighborhood into a greener place to live. The soil is happier because of all the nutrients you feed it, the vegetables are sweeter because you take the time to care for them, and guess what else? All the little bits you do to help Earth stay green and healthy may inspire other people to do their little bit to help. And then other people will inspire other people, and before you know it one little bit of help could turn into a tumbleweed of inspiration across the block, across the nation, across the world, and on and on like that.

**DyAnne DiSalvo**'s community spirit touches all the books she has written and illustrated for children, including *Uncle Willie and the Soup Kitchen, City Green, Grandpa's Corner Store,*

A *Castle on Viola Street*, and *Spaghetti Park*. She is the rhythm guitarist for the pop-rock band Smash Palace.

## WHAT YOU CAN DO!

When you have an idea, share it! Tell your best friend or your teacher or your state representative. One idea can change the world.

# POOP POWER

## By Barbara Seuling

My house in Vermont runs on cow power. Our gas and electric company in Vermont—dairy farm country—is one of the first in the United States to turn cow manure into energy. For a few dollars more on their bill each month, customers can choose to have their electricity come from cows.

The cows don't have to do anything except what comes naturally. Farmers collect their manure and store it in concrete bunkers underground, called digesters, where it ferments until it reaches 101 degrees. The gas released by the manure is burned to create enough power to run the entire farm.

The waste that's left is drained, and the liquids are used to fertilize crops, while the solids are turned into clean sawdust-like bedding for the cows—all smelling a lot better than in their original state—and the cycle begins all over again. This amounts to considerable savings of money and resources for the farmer and may even supplement his income, as he sells any excess energy to the local power company.

I thought this was a pretty cool example of recycling until I heard about San Francisco, home to a large population of environmentally conscious people and about 120,000 dogs. A waste company there has found a way to transform dog poop into energy!

Remember that fairy tale in which Rumpelstiltskin spun the lowliest form of plant life, straw, into the most valuable resource, gold? That seemed like pure fantasy once upon a time, but not so much anymore, when we're turning poop into power!

**Barbara Seuling** lights and heats her Vermont cottage with cow power, which helped her as she wrote more than four dozen books, including several about third grader Robert Dorfman.

# Eating Locally and Seasonally

## By Henry Winkler and Lin Oliver

Did you know that the average tomato travels fifteen hundred miles before it gets to your dining room table? Poor tomato; while it's riding in the back of the truck, it never even gets to look out the window. And how about this fact: Most of the fruits and vegetables you eat travel farther to get to you than you travel on your family vacation. We ask you, is it fair that a head of lettuce travels all the way across the country and you don't even get to go to Disney World?

Eating foods that are grown or raised far away from where you live is very bad for the environment. It wastes a tremendous amount of gas and energy to transport and preserve these foods before they get to you. We could conserve all this energy if we learned to eat locally, seasonally, and sustainably.

That means you should shop for foods that are grown in your area and you should eat foods when they are in season. This is not only good for the planet, it's also delicious fun.

Most communities have farmers' markets where local farmers sell what they grow. Both of us are farmers' market fans. We really enjoy exploring all the different stands and tasting the wonderful produce that was just pulled right out of the ground. What's better than eating a fresh, juicy, sweet white peach, especially when you've been waiting for it all winter long? How great to know that you can help the environment and throw your taste buds a party at the same time.

When not writing books for the series Hank Zipzer: The World's Greatest Underachiever, **HENRY WINKLER** and **LIN OLIVER** spend a lot of time cruising around their local farmers' markets, tasting all the seasonal delights.

# My savings save the world

## By Caroline B. Cooney

I don't buy or drink water in bottles. American towns and cities have excellent water, and it's usually fluoridated, essential for strong teeth, and you won't get that in bottled water. Buying water in plastic bottles just adds to the debris lying around.

I don't use a clothes dryer very often but hang things on a rack and an indoor line.

I keep the heat in the house rather low during the day and really low at night. I like wearing layers to stay warm.

I try not to buy food with lots of stiff plastic packaging. If I want crackers and cheese, I have crackers and cheese. I don't buy the little snack arrangements.

I'm lucky because our "downtown" is only two blocks

away and there are sidewalks. I walk to town every day to buy a few groceries, get a little fresh air, have some exercise, see the neighbors, avoid the car.

But these are tiny dents in my own life, never mind the world. I think many of us don't take such measures because, clearly, savings of energy are minuscule. I tell myself that there are three hundred million people in America, and if all three hundred million of us do an errand on foot instead of in the car, there will be savings that matter.

**CAROLINE B. COONEY** is the bestselling and award-winning author of numerous books, including *The Face on the Milk Carton*, *Code Orange*, *Goddess of Yesterday*, *A Friend at Midnight*, and *Diamonds in the Shadow*.

# The World—Our Home

## By Ben Mikaelsen

I live my life by one rule, always asking this question: Whatever I do, every minute of every day, if everybody in the world were doing that same thing, would it be a better world or a worse world? The answer to that question always guides my actions well. As an example, if I have something as small as a gum wrapper and nobody is around, throwing that small bit of garbage on the ground seems insignificant. But if six billion people around the world all did that same small act, it would instantly fill up a whole landfill. That would be tragic, and so I choose not to commit that simple act.

This sense of responsibility does not offer precise methods to help our Earth, but by adopting this attitude, you can realize how significant your choices and actions are in everything you do, every second and every minute of every day. As members of mankind, we have such a tremendous potential to destroy ourselves, but we also have a tremendous ability to make this world a wonderful home. To make it a good home, we must realize how important our collective behavior is. It is simple. It begins with the next decision you make and the next movement your body makes. What are you choosing to do?

**BEN MIKAELSEN** has won the International Reading Association Award, the Western Writers of America Golden Spur Award, and many state readers' medals. His novels include *Rescue Josh McGuire*, *Sparrow Hawk Red*, *Stranded*, *Countdown*, *Petey*, *Touching Spirit Bear*, *Red Midnight*, *Tree Girl*, and *Ghost of Spirit Bear*.

# GET INFORMATION! GET INVOLVED! GET GREEN!

Okay, enough reading. Now it's time to *do* something! Here are some Web sites you can visit to see what you can do to change the world.

**EPA Global Warming Kids site** (www.epa.gov/globalwarming/kids)
Learn about the greenhouse effect, how humans change the climate, and what we can do about it. This site has some games, too.

**What's Up with the Weather** (www.pbs.org/wgbh/warming)
This PBS site looks at global warming. Find out how much fossil fuel you use.

**The Green Squad** (www.nrdc.org/greensquad)
Kids taking action to make greener, healthier schools.

**Minnesota Pollution Control Agency Kids' Page**
(www.pca.state.mn.us/kids)
Lots of information about the environment here, and cool stuff like "creature of the month," coloring pages, and a students' guide to environmental information.

**Environmental Kids Club** (www.epa.gov/kids)
A club for kids interested in learning more about the environment and getting involved in environmental activities.

**Tree Musketeers** (www.treemusketeers.org)

An organization dedicated to empowering young people to lead movements for environmental improvement.

**It's Getting Hot in Here** (www.itsgettinghotinhere.org)

A growing movement of student and youth leaders who aim to stop global warming and build a more just and sustainable future.

**The Story of Stuff** (www.storyofstuff.com)

This is a terrific twenty-minute film about where our stuff comes from, what happens to it when we throw it away, and what we need to do to break the chain.

**National Geographic Kids** (www.kids.nationalgeographic.com/)

The online version of the popular magazine.

**Natural Resources Defense Council** (www.nrdc.org)

The council works to protect the planet—its people, plants, and animals—and to help create a new way of life for humankind, without fouling or depleting the resources that support all life on Earth.

**The Sierra Club** (www.sierraclub.org)

Founded in 1892, this is America's oldest, largest, and most influential environmental organization. More than a million members work to protect the planet.

**Greenpeace** (www.greenpeace.org/usa)

Since 1971, Greenpeace has been fighting to ban commercial whaling, convince the world's leaders to stop nuclear testing, protect

Antarctica, stop global warming, prevent the destruction of ancient forests, and avoid the threat of a nuclear disaster.

### Environmental Defense (www.environmentaldefense.org)

Founded in 1967 as the Environmental Defense Fund, this organization looks for innovative, practical ways to solve the most urgent environmental problems.

### Stop Global Warming (www.stopglobalwarming.org)

A movement to demand that our leaders reduce carbon dioxide emissions.

### The Green Guide (www.thegreenguide.com)

A resource from *National Geographic* for people striving toward a healthy and greener lifestyle. You'll find information about practical, everyday, environmentally responsible, and health-minded product choices and actions.

### Earth 911 (www.earth911.org)

Information about recycling centers, green shopping, green living, energy conservation, beach water quality, household hazardous waste, environmental education, composting, and more.

### Earth Day Network (www.earthday.net)

Founded by the organizers of the first Earth Day in 1970, Earth Day Network (EDN) promotes environmental citizenship and year-round environmental awareness.

### Earth Day in Your Neighborhood
(www.allspecies.org/neigh/block.htm)
How to observe Earth Day on your block.


For information about eating food grown locally and, in general, eating in a way that helps the environment, check out:
*www.100milediet.org*
*www.foodroutes.org*
*www.locavores.com*
*www.slowfoodusa.org*

### Green travel (www.ecotravel.com or www.ecotourismce.org)
Instead of going to some fake, plastic theme park this year, go on a *real* vacation and learn about the planet while you're doing it. Take nothing but pictures. Leave nothing but footprints.

### FreeSharing (www.freesharing.org)
Also known as free recycling or freecycling. A great way to find a new home for perfectly good stuff you don't want anymore, and to find cool stuff you want. If we swap things, they don't end up in the trash.

### Greendisk (www.greendisk.com)
You know all those hundreds of old videotapes your family never watches? These folks recycle them. They also take diskettes, Zip disks, CDs, CD-Rs, DVDs, cassettes, game cartridges, and virtually any other type of technotrash.

### Recycle all your electronics (www.computertakeback.com)
Don't throw old computer and TV equipment in the garbage. These folks will show you how to dispose of them safely.

### ClimateCounts (www.climatecounts.org)

Do you want to know which companies are green and which aren't? This is the place to go. Buy green!

### TreeHugger (www.treehugger.com)

A one-stop shop for green news, solutions, and product information.

### Play It Again Sports (www.playitagainsports.com)

This company buys and sells used sporting equipment. Don't throw away your old bats, balls, and hockey sticks. Find a new home for them! Play It Again Sports has nearly four hundred locations.

### Save gas! (www.fueleconomy.gov)

Tell your parents to learn how to drive! This site tells which cars get the best (and worst) gas mileage and shows how drivers can squeeze every last mile out of a gallon of gas. Did you know that every five miles per hour faster than sixty is like paying an extra twenty cents for each gallon of gas?

# ACKNOWLEDGMENTS

All the authors in this collection donated their time and words because they feel this is such an important cause. Please visit their Web sites and read their books.

We gratefully acknowledge the following for permission to use their work in this book.

"What Do I Do to Help Save the Environment?" © 2009 by Seymour Simon • "The Ugly Truth About Spit" © 2009 by Gennifer Choldenko • "A Few Small Steps" © 2009 by Rich Wallace • "Confessions of a Catalogaholic" © 2009 by Libba Bray • "Hanging Out" © 2009 by Lois Lowry • "One-Yard Penalty for Clipping" © 2009 by David Lubar • "Drinking Dog Water" © 2009 by Peg Kehret • "Cold Pizza for Breakfast" © 2009 by Jane Yolen • "Be a Superhero" © 2009 by Eoin Colfer • "Paperback Writer" © 2009 by Joseph Bruchac • "Turn It Off!" © 2009 by Eric A. Kimmel • "Since We Can't Stop Moose from Belching" © 2009 by Todd Strasser • "Celebrate Arbor Day!" © 2009 by Katy Kelly • "The Hoax" © 2009 by Gary Schmidt • "There Is No Meat in Chocolate Cake" © 2009 by Maryrose Wood • "Green and Gracious" © 2009 by Kirby Larson • "The Joy of Worm Composting" © 2009 by Ralph Fletcher • "I'm Green" © 2009 by David A. Adler • "Plunger-Man" © 2009 by Gordon Korman • "I Zapped My TV Set!" © 2009 by Bruce Coville • "Living in the City" © 2009 by Elizabeth Levy • "Be Passive!" © 2009 by Gail Gibbons • "Wrong Century" © 2009 by Debbie Dadey • "My House Has Vampires!" © 2009 by Megan McDonald • "Green . . . and Greener" © 2009 by Cynthia DeFelice • "Your Pick" © 2009 by Gail Carson Levine • "The Garbologist" © 2009 by Matt Tavares • "Zeus Says: Zap This!" ©

266